W9-CJE-292

ELEUTHÉRIA
A play in three acts

By Samuel Beckett
Translated from the French by Michael Brodsky

Foxrock, Inc./New York

© 1995 Les Editions de Minuit
English translation © 1995 Foxrock, Inc.
Published by permission of the Beckett Estate.

Introduction © 1995 S.E. Gontarski
Foreword © 1995 Martin Garbus
Translator's notes © 1995 Michael Brodsky

Published in the United States by:
Foxrock, Inc.
61 Fourth Avenue
New York, N.Y., 10003

Distributed by arrangement with Four Walls Eight Windows, Inc.

First printing May 1995

LIBRARY OF CONGRESS CATALOGING-IN-PUBLICATION DATA:
Beckett, Samuel, 1906
[Eleuthéria. English]
Eleuthéria/by Samuel Beckett
p. cm.
ISBN 0-9643740-0-5
I. Title.
PQ2603.E378E413   1995
842'.914—dc20   95-5229
CIP

Text design by Raugust Communications

Printed in the United States

10 9 8 7 6 5 4 3 2 1

FOREWORD

By Martin Garbus, Esq.

The dispute between the Beckett Estate and Foxrock over the publication of *Eleuthéria* is a clash of moral and legal values, personalities, cultures and legal systems.

Under French law, there is substantial protection of an author's moral rights to control his own work during his life and after death; in America, there is less protection. In America, because of the First Amendment, there is an extraordinary commitment to the free exchange of ideas; in case of doubt, we say publish and let the reader judge the value of the art.

Under the laws of France, the executor of an estate can decide which of the author's works can be published, if the author's intention is unclear.

In France, if the executor went to Court, and if the facts prove the author's intention changed and is unclear, then the executor's single voice could stop publication. In America, more weight would be given to the possible right of the public to read the work.

Rosset, a close friend and confidant to Beckett, was for thirty-three years the American publisher and dramatic agent for Beckett's work. He was responsible for the publication of over twenty volumes of Beckett's works as well as for approving performances of Beckett's works in the United States.

When Foxrock, the firm created to publish *Eleuthéria* by Rosset, John Oakes and Dan Simon, and

Jérôme Lindon, literary executor of the Beckett Estate, failed to agree whether and how the play should be published, I suggested three courses of action. The first suggestion was that the two sides in the dispute agree to appoint a third party or appoint two representatives to appoint a third party to decide if the facts permit publication. Lindon refused this proposal.

I then suggested that, in addition to potential third party arbitrators, there are groups of scholars and theater people, including the Samuel Beckett Society, that could play a role in resolving the dispute. Lindon refused to consider this possibility.

Finally, I suggested a variety of informal procedures. Lindon refused them all. This left us the option of resorting to more formal mediation of arbitration procedures, either in the United States or France. Lindon refused these as well.

I suggested that if we were to litigate we should agree to a variety of neutral principles that reduce the time, cost and rancor of a federal lawsuit. Lindon refused to consider them. His only course continued to be to threaten a federal copyright suit.

Rosset, Oakes and Simon hoped that if Lindon saw a favorable response to the play he would permit its publication and production. Accordingly, in New York, in September of 1994, a private reading of the play was arranged. Directed by Peter Craze of Britain, it was to be put on at the New York Theatre Workshop, but Lindon threatened to sue the theater, Rosset, the translator and the actors if the reading took place.

The Theatre Workshop, caught in the middle, asked Rosset to post a $25,000 bond, which he could not do.

Following the precedent set by John House-
man and Orson Welles when their premiere of Marc
Blitzstein's *The Cradle Will Rock* was canceled by the
WPA Theater Project on what was to have been its
opening night in 1936, Foxrock changed the venue
for the reading and, with a group of 13 actors and an
audience of approximately 100 invited guests, a reading was conducted that very same day of the theater
cancellation in a rehearsal studio in the building
where Rosset lives.

Critics who saw the reading discussed the play's
substantial merits and its importance in the Beckett
oeuvre, and great interest in a future production was
aroused.

As a result of the reading and examination of
the manuscript, both in its original French and in a translation, letters were addressed to myself and to Foxrock
from some of America's most important and creative
stage directors and theater owners. They stated a deep
interest in the play; more importantly, many of those
who wrote stated that they wished to produce *Eleuthéria*
and that its performance would constitute a major theatrical event. Rosset told all the directors in advance
that they would have to obtain permission from the
Beckett Estate. Lindon received these letters and refused
permission and said he would not be persuaded by them.

Finally, Foxrock had me prepare papers to file
in Federal Court copyright action in the United States
District Court in New York, seeking an injunction and
declaratory judgment that the play could be published and performed. Lindon had threatened, if the
book were published, to sue bookstore owners and
book distributors in the same way that he threatened
the publishers of this book and the New York Theatre

Workshop that had offered to house the reading of the play. However, at this point, the publishers decided to bypass legal action and to proceed with the "publication" of *Eleuthéria* in a limited edition.

Rosset proposed this limited not-for-sale edition in order to make the book available to at least some of the people most interested in *Eleuthéria*. The publishers were taking a risk and they knew it, but the decision was made to publish. They were very aware that censorship of their efforts could come about through either governmental court action or expensive, time-consuming litigation. They went ahead. Thus, the forthcoming publication of the free edition of *Eleuthéria* was announced. A normal, commercial edition had been announced previously, but this new plan superseded it.

At that point, Lindon, apparently realizing the true determination of his American opponents, agreed to Foxrock's publication of *Eleuthéria*. He had done nearly all he could to prevent its publication, and seeing that it was futile, wrote to Rosset:

> ...[A]s I see you are staunchly bent on publishing your translation, I bring myself to grant you that publication right for the United States which you have been asking me for two years...The one thing I am sure of is that Sam would not have liked us to fight against each other about him in a public lawsuit. My decision — I should say: renouncing — is essentially due to that.

And so, this edition at long last brings to the public the text of an important play that for too long has been read only by a handful of privileged scholars.

We hope and believe this edition will eventually lead to the play's performance.

The play's title, *Eleuthéria,* is a Greek word meaning "freedom."

INTRODUCTION

By S.E. Gontarski

"Perhaps it is time that someone were simply nothing"
—Victor Krap

In his catalogue of the Samuel Beckett papers at the University of Texas's Humanities Research Center, Carlton Lake calls attention to the curious publishing history of the work Samuel Beckett wrote just after World War II as he turned to writing in French: "Along with *Watt* and *Mercier et Camier* one of the more long-drawn-out publishing histories in Beckett's career is that leading up to *Nouvelles et textes pour rien*" (i.e., *Stories and Texts for Nothing*).[1] Indeed, this was a period in Beckett's creative life when the time between composition and publication was unusually protracted. *Watt,* for instance, written mostly in the south of France during the Second World War and completed in 1945, did not see print for some eight years after its completion. It was rejected by more publishers than even Beckett could remember before being published by the group Beckett called the "*Merlin* juveniles" in collaboration with Maurice Girodias's notorious Olympia Press in 1953. Beckett's short story "Suite" (later "La Fin" or "The End") was finished in May 1946. It was published almost immediately in the July 1946 issue of *Les Temps Modernes.* Beckett expected the second half of the story to appear in the October issue, but Simone de Beauvoir considered the first part complete in itself and refused to publish the second. Beckett argued that print-

ing half the story was a "mutilation," but Mme. de
Beauvoir remained adamant, and it was some nine
years before the complete story appeared. Beckett in
fact wrote four French stories, *nouvelles*, in 1946, and
he expected that they would appear quickly in book
form from his first French publisher, Bordas, which
would publish his own translation of *Murphy* in 1947.
By December of 1946 Beckett could write with some
confidence to his English friend and agent, George
Reavey, "I hope to have a book of short stories ready
for the spring (in French). I do not think that I shall
write very much in English in the future."[2] But Bordas
dropped plans to issue both *Mercier et Camier* and the
four stories, *Quatre Nouvelles*, when sales of the French
Murphy proved disastrous. When Beckett finally found
a second French publisher willing to take on the
whole of his creative backlog, Les Editions de Minuit,
in 1950, he hesitated and finally withheld much of
the earliest writing in French, *Mercier et Camier*, one
of his four stories, "First Love," and his first full-length
play written in French, *Eleuthéria*. The remaining
three nouvelles of 1946 were finally published in
France by Les Editions de Minuit in 1955 and in the
U. S. by Grove Press in 1967, both in combination
with 13 *Texts for Nothing*. Both *Mercier et Camier* and
"First Love" were eventually published as Beckett
yielded to pressure from his publishers: 1970 in
French and 1974 in English.

  But these publishing difficulties, hiatuses, hesitations, instances of self-doubt and self-censorship
pale before the intractable difficulties surrounding
the publication of Beckett's first full-length play,
Eleuthéria, published only in 1995, nearly half a century after its writing. If the publication history of *Watt*,

Mercier et Camier, and "Première Amour" is curious, the history of *Eleuthéria* is curiouser. As with *Mercier et Camier* and his four *Stories,* Beckett was at first eager to have *Eleuthéria* performed and published. He saw *Eleuthéria* as part of a sequence which reflected a certain continuity to his writing. On July 8, 1948, for example, he wrote to George Reavey, "I am now typing, for rejection by the publishers, *Malone meurt* [*Malone Dies*], the last I hope of the series *Murphy, Watt, Mercier & Camier, Molloy,* not to mention the 4 nouvelles & *Eleuthéria.*"[3] *Malone Dies* was not, of course, the last of the series. Another play followed shortly thereafter, *En Attendant Godot* (*Waiting for Godot*), completed in January of 1949, and a third French novel, *L'innommable* (*The Unnamable*), completed a year later. Along with *Molloy* and *Malone Dies, The Unnamable* formed part of what Beckett called "the so-called Trilogy."

Eleuthéria was begun on January 18, 1947 as a retreat from the problems caused by the prose Beckett had been writing at the time. As he told his first biographer Deirdre Bair in 1972, "I turned to writing plays to relieve myself from the awful depression the prose led me into. Life at the time was too demanding, too terrible, and I thought theatre would be a diversion."[4] By February 24 he had completed a draft of the three-act play, and by late March 1947 he had turned over a typescript (which he always made himself, mindful perhaps of the errors and changes introduced into James Joyce's work by various typists) to Toni Clerkx, sister of Bram and Geer van Velde, who would for a time function as Beckett's literary representative in France, and who was responsible for placing *Murphy* with Bordas. And in fact Mme. Clerkx managed to

interest Jean Vilar at the Théâtre Nationale Populaire
in the play, but Vilar wanted Beckett to cut it to one
long act. When Beckett refused, Vilar dropped his
interest. By the fall of 1947, Mme. Clerkx told Beckett
that she could no longer represent him and still have
time for her own writing, and so Beckett's live-in com-
panion and future wife, Suzanne Descheveaux-
Dumesnil, began to circulate his work among pro-
ducers and publishers.

By January of 1949, Beckett had completed a
second French play, *En attendant Godot* (*Waiting for
Godot*), written again "as a relaxation to get away from
the awful prose I was writing at the time," this time
presumably *Molloy* and *Malone meurt* (*Malone Dies*),
and that play too was circulated by Mme.
Descheveaux-Dumesnil—without success, until she
saw a production of August Strindberg's *Ghost Sonata*
performed at the Gaité Montparnasse in early spring
of 1950. The play, staged by Roger Blin, a disciple of
Antonin Artaud, had impressed her, and she dropped
the typescripts of both plays at the box office for Blin
to consider. Blin had heard of Beckett from the Dada
poet Tristan Tzara. He was interested in the plays even
though "he frankly did not understand *Waiting for
Godot*, but he liked it. He decided that he should probably begin with *Eleuthéria* because it was more tradi-
tional, and to his mind easier to cope with."[5] But finally economics entered the decision-making process,
and as Blin noted, "*Eleuthéria* had seventeen characters, a divided stage, elaborate props and complicated
lighting. I was poor. I didn't have a penny. I couldn't
think of anyone who owned a theater suitable for such
a complicated production. I thought I'd be better
off with *Godot* because there were only four actors

and they were bums. They could wear their own clothes if it came to that, and I wouldn't need anything but a spotlight and a bare branch for a tree." With such decisions, then, was theater history shaped.

In October of 1950 Suzanne Descheveaux-Dumesnil, still systematically and assiduously making the rounds of French publishers, delivered the typescripts of three novels, the "so-called trilogy," *Molloy*, *Malone meurt* and *L'innommable*, to the desk of Georges Lambrich, an editor at Jérôme Lindon's Editions de Minuit, a house rapidly gaining a reputation among the Paris avant-garde. By November, Beckett had a French publisher, and the publication of *Molloy* was scheduled for January of 1951 (although it was finally delayed several months) to be followed shortly thereafter by *Malone meurt*. Blin had been making some headway with the production of *Waiting for Godot*. He had interested Jean-Marie Serreau in the play just as Serreau was opening his Théâtre de Babylone, and Blin had gotten a small grant from the French Ministry for Arts and Letters to produce the play. Jérôme Lindon had seen copies of the two plays and had agreed to publish them as well, provided that he was not broke himself by then, and the two plays along with the third novel of the trilogy were then announced as forthcoming in the pages of Beckett's first two French novels, *Molloy* and *Malone meurt*. By June 1953 Beckett had an American publisher, Barney Rosset, of the fledgling Grove Press, about which "Sylvia Beach said very nice things,"[6] and a "first version of [the English] *Godot*" was "in the hands of Mr. Harold L. Oram, 8 West 40th Street, New York, who has our authority to treat for the performance rights up till I think November 1st." The recognition that

Beckett had sought for so long was now in reach, and he pursued it—but not without hesitations. He withdrew from publication *Mercier et Camier,* "First Love," and the play that bears a curious relationship to "First Love," *Eleuthéria,* which he then consistently withheld from publication and performance.

Although *Eleuthéria* sat in Beckett's trunk, it was not exactly an unknown work. Beckett destroyed neither typescripts nor manuscript notebooks. In fact they were finally sold or donated to major research libraries, namely the Humanities Research Center at the University of Texas, which holds the two manuscript notebooks, Dartmouth College, which holds the original typescript, and Washington University, St. Louis, and the University of Reading (Reading, England), each of which holds a copy of the typescript. Individual copies had also circulated freely among Beckett scholars as a sort of *samizdat* network once Beckett attracted sufficient reputation among academics in the late 1950s, and a number of important studies of Beckett's dramatic works have included essays on *Eleuthéria.*[7] By 1986, Beckett had relented somewhat on his ban against the play's publication. He allowed a significant portion of it, almost a third of it, to be published in France as part of a tribute volume to honor his eightieth birthday, in the special issue of *Revue d'Esthétique.*[8] And several pages were published in *Beckett in the Theatre:* the dialogue between the Glazier and his son, of which Beckett has said, "the source of the dialogue between the boy and Vladimir [in *Waiting for Godot*] is to be found in the unpublished play *Eleuthéria.*"[9]

In fact, in the spring of 1986 Beckett was on the verge once again of releasing the whole of

Eleuthéria to his long-time friend and American publisher Barney Rosset. That spring, Parisians were honoring the eightieth birthday of their adopted son, Samuel Beckett. The great museum of modern art in Paris, the Centre Pompidou, sponsored a week-long celebration of Beckett's work with lectures, exhibits, discussions, and performances. The massive special issue of the *Revue d'Esthétique* appeared in the windows of most of the city's bookshops in time for the Pompidou festivities. Beckett himself, slightly embarrassed by the attention, kept his distance, absenting himself, as was his habit, even from performances of his work. He met with friends quietly as they came into town at the café of the Hôtel PLM not far from his Boulevard St. Jacques apartment, but he spent most of the time buried in the "Marne mud" of his Ussy retreat. On his birthday, however, he was back in Paris and attended a small reception at one of his old haunts, La Coupole, which he had avoided for over two decades, preferring the Falstaff around the corner and finally the hygienic anonymity and privacy of the Hôtel PLM.

As a group of us sipped drinks at the Bar Américain, Beckett's American publisher, Barney Rosset, came through the doors in a flurry announcing that he had been discharged from the company he built and ran for over thirty-three years, Grove Press. The mood of the evening shifted. It seemed impossible that Rosset could be separated from Grove; in our minds, of course, they were one. Rosset *was* Grove Press. But he had sold it a year earlier in an effort to recapitalize. The new owners, Ann Getty and Lord Weidenfeld, had pledged to keep Rosset on for five years as Editor-in-Chief — or so he thought.

One clause of his contract stipulated that Rosset actually served at the pleasure of the new owners, and they were displeased, particularly at Rosset's chronic inability to adapt to the corporate structure. We sipped our drinks and shook our heads, grumbling that if the decision to publish Beckett rested with boards of directors, rather than visionary publishers like Rosset and Lindon, and was based on marketing surveys, he would have remained an unpublished writer.

Beckett arrived—rather materialized—promptly at eight. No one saw him come in. Suddenly, he was just standing there in a grey, outsized greatcoat and brown beret. We greeted him and withdrew to a cluster of tables in the corner of the cordoned bar area where Beckett was briefed on the Rosset affair. What could be done, he queried. Rosset shrugged his shoulders and muttered, more into the table that to anyone in particular, "Start over, I guess." It was immediately clear from the tenor of the conversation that for Beckett also Rosset was Grove Press. It was Barney Rosset who was Samuel Beckett's American publisher, not some corporate entity called Grove Press. Years later, John Calder would call Rosset Beckett's "spiritual son," and on that snowy April evening Beckett responded much like a spiritual father. Perhaps he might find something in the trunk to help Rosset begin yet again.

Rosset and Beckett met several times during the week to work out details. The obvious choice was for Rosset to publish *Dream of Fair to Middling Women*, the unfinished English novel of 1932 which Beckett later plundered for two of the stories in *More Pricks Than Kicks*.[10] But *Dream* remained a sensitive work for Beckett in 1986. It featured a protagonist who was only a thinly disguised alter-ego of the author, and it was a *roman à clef*. Some of its models were still alive and would surely be embarrassed by its publication. Beckett finally settled on his first full-length play, *Eleuthéria*. He inscribed a copy of the play to Rosset to seal the agreement, and withdrew to Ussy to take on the clearly distasteful task of translating the play into English.

Although he is listed as the translator into English or French on almost all of his work, Beckett never was strictly a translator of himself. Each shift in language produced not a literary or linguistic equivalent but a new work. Beckett's translations have always been transformations, a continuation of the creative process. There simply are no equivalents between Beckett's French and English texts. Theater, moreover, required yet another major transformation, a reconceptualization of the work for stage space. During his twenty-year career as a theatrical director, from 1967-1986, Beckett seized any opportunity to review his plays to continue the creative process. As a theatrical director of his own work he at least revised and at times rewrote every play he directed. The task of translating *Eleuthéria* was not as simple as it at first sounded.

It came as little surprise, then, that shortly after Beckett began the task, he abandoned it as too taxing in his eightieth year. It would have meant recreating a play he wrote some four decades earlier. Rosset was no more disappointed than Beckett himself, but Beckett offered some consolation—three short new prose works which he called *Stirrings Still* and which he dedicated to Rosset.

Rosset, however, never abandoned plans to publish *Eleuthéria*. A draconian contract with the new owners of the press forbid his competing with Grove directly, and the publication of *Eleuthéria* would have violated at least the spirit if not the letter of that agreement. But after Grove Press changed hands yet again, Rosset resumed plans to publish *Eleuthéria* in English. On March 3, 1993, he wrote to Beckett's literary executor, the French publisher Jérôme Lindon, to inform him that he was making plans to publish the work that Beckett had offered him in 1986: " . . . It is now time to publish *Eleuthéria,* and I hope that we can do so in cooperation with each other and avoid the confusion, misunderstandings, in-fighting, and legal battles surrounding the publication of *Dream of Fair to Middling Women.*"

Lindon's initial reply on March 5, 1993 suggested some room for negotiation. While insisting on Samuel Beckett's *interdictum* on *Eleuthéria,* Lindon nevertheless suggested, "I do not believe that much in everlasting perpetuity of steadfast stand-points. It is likely that *Eleuthéria* might be published some day, in some way or other, in French first, then in other languages. When? I cannot possibly tell you for the time being." Rosset continued preparations to publish the play while negotiations proceeded, commissioning a second translation from Albert Bermel and taking on a co-publisher, John Oakes and Dan Simon's Four Walls Eight Windows; together they formed the company Foxrock, Inc. through which to publish the play. The negotiations between the two strong-willed publishers, however, grew increasingly acrimonious. The conflict was unfortunate in a number of respects, not the least of which was that the two most important figures in Samuel Beckett's publishing life were at loggerheads with each other, and both were acting out of the firm conviction that they had Samuel Beckett's best interests at heart. Lindon as best he could was trying to fulfill Samuel Beckett's final wishes to the letter. Rosset was acting through the historical imperative that had driven his thirty-three years at Grove Press, that major work by major writers should not be suppressed or limited to an élite that had privileged access to it. Rosset's attitude toward *Eleuthéria* was no different from his attitude toward *Lady Chatterley's Lover* or the *Tropic of Cancer*, except that Samuel Beckett offered the play to him directly in 1986. Beckett was fiercely loyal to his original publishers. In fact to demonstrate his confidence in Rosset, Beckett made formal in a letter of February 1, 1986, an agreement that they had between them informally: "This is to confirm that I have appointed you my exclusive theatrical agent for North America. This agreement shall remain in effect until such time as either one of us decides to terminate it."

In fact, when Rosset took on Samuel Beckett as a Grove author, Beckett warned him in a letter dated June 25, 1953 of the implications involved in publishing his work:

> I hope you realize what you are letting yourself in for. I do not mean the heart of the matter, which is unlikely to disturb anybody, but certain obscenities of form which may not have struck you in French as they will in English, and which frankly (it is better that you should know this before we get going) I am not at all disposed to mitigate. I do not of course realize what is possible in America from this point of view and what is not. Certainly, as far as I know such passages, faithfully translated, would not be tolerated in England.[11]

Both publishers by then had taken considerable risks with Samuel Beckett's work, financial and legal, and Beckett was intensely loyal to both, making Jérôme Lindon finally his literary executor and trying to insure Barney Rosset's future by offering him his last major unpublished work for publication.

In September 1994 Rosset decided to bring the play to the attention of a broader audience by offering a public reading in New York. Samuel Beckett's nephew, Edward, denounced the action to the *New York Times,* suggesting that "all those who may be party to this New York event [i.e., the play's reading] which deliberately transgresses the will expressed by Samuel Beckett, would of course expose themselves to legal proceedings." That threat was enough to scare off the New York Theater Workshop, where the reading was originally scheduled to take place. Undeterred by the theater's failure of nerve, Rosset gathered the audience outside the New York Theater Workshop and led them through the streets of New York, a procession in search of an author, to his apartment building, where space was found for the reading. By November 22, 1994 the acrimony had increased. Rosset had been discharged as Beckett's theatrical agent, and Lindon wrote to co-publishers John G.H. Oakes and Dan Simon:

> In order to avoid any ambiguity, I made a point of warning Barney Rosset by return post that should he publish *Eleuthéria* then the Beckett estate would prosecute not only the publishers but all those—translators and distributors, among others—who have been accessory to that illicit action.

At this point of maximum conflict, when it looked as though the only resolution to this drama would be a protracted court battle, the issues were resolved. A third translation was commissioned from the novelist Michael Brodsky, and Lindon prepared to publish the play in French before its English appearance. The "Avertissement" to his edition makes clear, however, that he was publishing the work against his better judgment since Beckett considered it *"une pièce ratée"* (a failed play).

Rosset's position was that such judgments are best left to history. Beckett had often been overly critical of his own work. In the letter to Rosset dated February 11, 1954, for example, Beckett noted, "It's hard to go on with everything loathed and repudiated as soon as formulated, and in the act of formulation, and before formulation." In the same letter, Beckett noted that he has had to resist Lindon's pressure to publish another *oeuvre inachevée:* "[Lindon] also wanted to publish *Mercier et Camier,* the first 'novel' in French and of which the less said the better, but I had to refuse." It is our good fortune that Jérôme Lindon persisted and finally prevailed, and Minuit published *Mercier et Camier* in 1970, Grove in 1974. It is to our good fortune as well that Beckett's two major publishers came to an agreement about the publication of *Eleuthéria.*

To Lindon's mind, *"tous les vrais connaisseurs de son travail que j'ai connus considéraient* Eleuthéria *comme une pièce ratée. "* And critics like Ruby Cohn have agreed. But how successful *Eleuthéria* is as a play (*qua* play) may not be exactly the right question to ask about its publication. Carlton Lake, for one, places the focus on the work's historical significance: "It is a late-blooming transitional work and, even though preceded by other works in French, forms a bridge between Beckett the English language writer and Beckett the French writer."[12] And in what is perhaps the most comprehensive essay written on the play, Dougald McMillan writes:

> [*Eleuthéria*] was thus the culmination of [Beckett's] examination of the dramatic tradition of which he was a part. If we do not have for Beckett a direct manifesto like Corneille's *First Discourse on the Uses and Elements of Dramatic Poetry*, Strindberg's prefaces to *Miss Julie* and *A Dream Play*, Zola's preface to *Thérèse Raquin*, or Brecht's *Short Organum for the Theater*, we do have in *Eleuthéria* Beckett's own full statement on dramatic method—a statement which clearly influenced his later plays.[13]

There is no question that Beckett was not happy finally with this play and that he had not fully solved all its dramatic problems, and so could not translate it when he tried. It is after all a drama in the throes of resisting becoming a drama. Beckett wrote a play in which the main character refuses to or simply cannot explain the very motives of his action, which motives have traditionally driven the machinery of drama, his desire to be nothing. With *Eleuthéria*, Beckett was learning to risk absence on the stage, to empty the theatrical space, first of motive, then of character. It would take another play before he would solve this dramatic problem of presenting "nothing" by removing one of the central characters from the stage—Godot. *Eleuthéria* is not there yet, but it shows the way. It may be only, say, Krap's first tape, which of course is less developed, less complete than Krapp's last tape. But *Eleuthéria* is the beginning of "it all." It already anticipates the apparitions of the later work. And chronologically nearer, we can see as well the novel *Molloy* evolving from Victor's futile struggles to explain himself. But *Eleuthéria* has its own qualities as well, and it is now in the hands of a broader public to decide if and how it fails, if and how it succeeds.

Notes

1. *No Symbols Where None Intended: A Catalogue of Books, Manuscripts, and Other Material Relating to Samuel Beckett in the Collections of the Humanities Research Center*, Selected and Described by Carlton Lake (Austin, TX: Humanities research Center, 1984), 81.

2. Carlton Lake, 81.

3. Carlton Lake, 53.

4. Deirdre Bair, *Samuel Beckett: A Biography* (New York: Summit Books, 1990), 361.

5. Deirdre Bair, 403.

6. S.B. letter to Barney Rosset, 25 June 1953, in *The Review of Contemporary Fiction* (Grove Press Issue), ed. by S. E. Gontarski, 10.3 (Fall 1990): 65.

7. See, for instance, Ruby Cohn, *Back to Beckett* (Princeton: Princeton University Press, 1973), 124-7; Guy Croussy, *Beckett* (Paris: Hachette, 1971), 102-3; John Fletcher and John Spurling *Beckett: A Study of His Plays* (New York: Hill and Wang, 1972), XX; James Knowlson and John Pilling, *Frescoes of the Skull: The Later Prose and Drama of Samuel Beckett* (New York: Grove Press, 1980), 23-38; and most importantly, Dougald McMillan and Martha Fehsenfeld, *Beckett in the Theatre: The Author as Practical Playwright and Director* (New York: Riverrun Press, 1988), 29-45.

8. Numéro hors-série (Paris: Editions Privat, 1986), 111-132. See also Dougald McMillan, "*Eleuthéria*: le Discours de la Méthode inédit de Samuel Beckett," translated by Edith Fournier, in the same issue, pp. 101-109.

9. *En attendant Godot*, edited by Colin Duckworth (London: George G. Harrap, 1966), xlv.

10. The novel finally appeared, amid much squabbling among its publishers, from Black Cat Press, Dublin, in 1992 and from Arcade Publishing, in association with Riverrun Press, in 1993, both editions edited by Eoin O'Brien and Edith Fournier. In his letter to the *Times Literary Supplement* on 16 July 1993, however, Eoin O'Brien dissociates himself from the second edition, although he remains listed as its editor: "Both the US (Arcade) and UK (Calder) 1993 editions of this work have been printed without taking into account the necessary corrections I, and my co-editor, Edith Fournier, made to the proofs of the re-set text. It is of deep concern that Samuel Beckett's work be treated in this manner. We can be held accountable," he continues, "only for the first edition published in 1992 by Black Cat Press in Dublin and can accept no responsibility for the errors in the US and UK flawed editions."

11. The whole of this letter is published in the Grove Press issue of *The Review of Contemporary Fiction*, pp. 64-5.

12. Carlton Lake, p. 51.

13. McMillan and Fehsenfeld, pp. 29-30.

TRANSLATOR'S NOTE

By Michael Brodsky

The process of translating *Eleuthéria* revealed over and over that preservation of meaning, both overarching and minute, from French to English, required an unswerving dedication to what I came to call "tonal value." Because this creature is so much a function of context, it was not unusual for the same word appearing in many different places in the French text to require starkly different equivalents in English.

Depending on the speaker and state of things on stage, a word like *histoire* (an *Eleuthéria* jack-of-all-trades) might mean "firsthand account," "business" or (as *chez* Mme. Meck) "a thing to happen!". Similarly, *formidable* seemed at one moment (Pioukian) best served by (a very self-aggrandizing) "tremendous" and at another (Glazierlike) by (a very other-deflating) "first-rate."

Although at some point the French *supprimer* (tonal value: penological, archly literary/legal) managed to survive its translantic flight "intact" (as "suppress," tonal value pretty much the same), its more offhand and everyday shading elsewhere demanded, alas, a less cognately configuration ("do away with") in English.

What became most conspicuous in the course of translating was, first, Beckett's fascination with shardlike colloquializings as (a) played against extended arias of abstraction — monologues on such topics as freedom: the ever-receding tortoise à la Zeno, the worker's relation to his/her raw materials, plausibility of a given theatrical system, the ups and downs of the euthanasia business, and humankind's unaccountable soft spot for its essential thwartedness on every front and (b) aiding and abetting, in contrast to problem-play psychologizing, brute duration's highly suggestive contamination of the life lived on stage.

Second, it became clear that Beckett's struggle with/resistance to creating the work was to be transmogrified into the very thew and sinew — the living fiber — of that work's unfolding over stage time; indeed, his unquenchable ambivalence about siring a protagonist whose plight might hold water in the audience-friendly "plane of the feasible" does get itself enacted, and through ever greater elaboration, compliments of the endearing teamwork of the conscientiously hideous Dr. Piouk, the conscientiously Mephistophelean Glazier and the conscientiously (and ebulliently) Pirandellian Audience member.

In my sojourn among them I've tried to respect their creator's predilection for building toward an extreme response to things as they are via the most uninflectedly basic of constituents.

In closing, I thank Laurence Brodsky for her crucial help.

ACKNOWLEDGEMENTS

By Barney Rosset

I would like to acknowledge, foremost and most importantly, John G.H. Oakes and Dan Simon, the intensely creative and energizing founders and publishers of Four Walls Eight Windows, Inc., which is the partner firm to Blue Moon Books, Inc. in Foxrock, Inc. Foxrock was named (and we feel properly named) after Samuel Beckett's birthplace, and was founded to publish *Eleuthéria*. Without John and Dan, the project would at best have been very dubious. They made it happen.

Stan Gontarski, whose combination of good academic research, keen observation and enthusiasm for the creative impulse in modern literature opened up this new pathway to Beckett.

Michael Brodsky and his consummate effort as the translator who came on board at a late and crucial moment with "full speed ahead" and "damn the torpedos."

Our English cohorts, Peter Craze, director, John Zeitler, his assistant, and James Stephens, actor, for their successful efforts in giving us a most memorable reading of *Eleuthéria*. They transformed detours into a main thoroughfare. Cristina Middleton (who found them) and the whole wonderful American cast which included: Keith Benedict, Laila Robins, Lola Pashalinski, Patricia Connelly, Edie Avioli, Emily Bly, Austin Pendleton, Richmond Hoxie, Scott Sears, Steven Petrasca, Lynn Cohen, and Doug Stender. Thanks to David Beyda, for his technical assistance. And another Brit, Pat Butcher, whose suggestions on many aspects, including, and especially, translation, were valued.

The Blue Moon staff: Louella Dizon, Iza Ostolski, Yvonne Pesquera and Richard Baxstrom, who all contributed their organizational skills, composure and *savoir faire* under fire.

And terribly important to me personally, my own *aide de camp*, Astrid Myers, whose wise counsel and unflagging belief in the cause never let me down.

And our valiant counselors at law, Martin Garbus and Robert Solomon who waved us through all red lights and stop signs. It was "Gung ho" from the start.

Our thanks to Albert Bermel, for his belief in and early work on the project; Beckett specialist Lois Oppenheim, and the writer, Deirdre Bair.

Joe Strick, my close friend for more than fifty years, was there encouraging and advising me at every step.

Samuel Beckett. Sam, you wrote to your friend Tom McGreevy in 1948. Speaking of *Eleuthéria* you said that "I think it will see the boards in time, even if only for a few nights." Well, Sam, all of us have done our best to make your prediction come true. *Eleuthéria,* as of this writing, is not yet "on the boards," but now you can count on the fact that it will be, and here is the most important evidence for that conclusion—*Eleuthéria* in book form. Sam, I would like to believe and I do believe that all of the outpouring of love and admiration for you and your work expressed by the people whom I have named, and those whom I have unwittingly left unnamed, would have pleased you. And so to you, Sam, God Bless!

ELEUTHÉRIA
A play in three acts

By Samuel Beckett
Translated from the French by Michael Brodsky

CAST OF CHARACTERS

M. Henri Krap.
Mme. Henri Krap.
Victor Krap, their son.
Madame Meck, friend of the Kraps'.
Dr. André Piouk.
Madame André Piouk, sister of Madame Krap.
Mademoiselle Olga Skunk, Victor's fiancée.
A Glazier.
Michel, his son.
An Audience member.
Tchoutchi, a Chinese torturer.
Madame Karl, Victor's landlady.
Jacques, manservant in the Krap home.
Marie, maidservant in the Krap home, Jacques's
fiancée.
Thomas, Madame Meck's chauffeur.
Joseph, a thug.
Prompter.

Place: Paris.
Time: Three successive winter afternoons.

This play, in the first two acts, calls for a staging juxtaposing two distinct locations and therefore two simultaneous actions, a main action and a marginal action, the latter silent apart from a few short sentences and, as regards non-verbal expression, reduced to the vague attitudes and movements of a single character. Strictly speaking, less an action than a site, often empty.

The script concerns the main action exclusively. The marginal action is the actor's business, within the limits of the directions in the following Note.

NOTE ON THE STAGE SET-UP AND THE MARGINAL ACTION

The scene on stage, in the first two acts, depicts, juxtaposed, two locales separated from each other in real space, namely, Victor's room and an area of the morning room at the Krap home, the latter as if wedged into the former. There is no partition. Victor's room moves imperceptibly on into the Kraps' morning room, as the sullied into the clean, the sordid into the decent, breadth into clutter. Over the entire width of the stage there is the same back wall, the same flooring, which, however, in moving on from Victor to his family, become housebroken and presentable. It's the high seas becoming the harbor basin. The question is therefore one of conveying scenically the sense of a dualistic space less via transition effects than through the fact that Victor's room takes up three quarters of the stage and by the flagrant disharmony between the two sets of furnishings, those of Victor's room comprising a folding bedstead and nothing more, those of the room at the Kraps' a highly elegant round table, four period chairs, an armchair, a floor lamp and a sconce.

The daytime lighting is the same for the two sides (window in the middle of the back wall). But each has its appropriate artificial lighting, Victor's (Acts II and III) the bulb provided by the Glazier, the Krap morning room's (Acts I and II) the floor lamp and, at the end of the first act, the sconce which stays lit after floor lamp is turned off.

Each side has its own door.

In each act Victor's room is presented from another angle, with the result that, viewed from the house, it is to the left of the Krap enclave in the first act, to the right of the Krap enclave in the second act, and that from one act to the next the main action remains on the right. This also explains why there is no marginal action in the third act, the Krap side having fallen into the pit following the swing of the scene on stage.

The main action and the marginal action never encroach, nor do they more than barely comment, on each other. The characters on the two sides are checked, in their movements toward each other, by the barrier they alone see. Which doesn't prevent them from almost touching at times. The marginal action, in the first two acts, has to be carried through with the utmost discretion. Most of the time it is a question only of a site and of a being in stasis. The rare unavoidable movements, with a function, like Madame Karl's entrance and Victor's exit in the first act, Victor's entrance and exit in the second act, and the two sentences (Madame Karl's in the first act, Jacques's in the second) are to be led in to through a sort of wavering in the main action, but then it often is wavering.

The marginal action occurs, in the first act in Victor's room, in the second in the Krap morning room.

Marginal Action, Act I

Victor in bed. Motionless. There is no need to see him at once. He moves this way and that, sits up in bed, gets up, goes back and forth, in his stocking feet, in every direction, from the window to the footlights, from the door to the invisible barrier on the main action side, slowly and vaguely, often stops, looks out the window, toward the audience, goes back to sit on the bed, gets back in bed, becomes motionless, gets up again, resumes his walk, etc. But he is more often motionless or moving this way and that in one spot than moving off. His movements, for all their vagueness, do follow just the same a most decided rhythm and pattern, so that one ends up knowing his position approximately without having to look at him.

At a certain point, namely when Madame Krap has had time to arrive, Madame Karl enters and says: *Your mother.* Victor seated on the bed. A silence. He gets up, looks for something (his shoes), doesn't find them, exits in his stocking feet. Room empty. Dimmer and dimmer. Victor returns after, say, five minutes, resumes his flim-flam. He is to be lying in bed, motionless, all through the end of the main action, involving Monsieur Krap and Jacques.

Marginal Action, Act II

Stage for a long time empty. Enter Jacques. He goes back and forth, exits. Stage again for a long time empty. Enter Jacques, he goes back and forth, exits. One senses that he is thinking of his master whose armchair he gently touches several times over. Stage again empty. Enter Jacques. He turns on the floor lamp, goes back and forth, exits. Stage again empty. At a certain point, namely when Victor has had time to arrive, Jacques shows him in. Victor sits down in his father's armchair, under the floor lamp. Victor a long time motionless. Enter Jacques. Jacques: *Monsieur may come along.* Victor gets up and exits. Stage empty until the end of the act.

ACT I

An area of the morning room in the home of the Kraps.

Round table, four period chairs, club chair, floor lamp, wall lamp with shade.

A late afternoon in winter.

Madame Krap seated at the table.

Madame Krap motionless.

A knock. A silence. Another knock.

MME. KRAP	(With a start) Come in. (Enter Jacques. He holds out to Mme. Krap a tray bearing a calling card. She takes up the card, looks at it, puts it back on the tray) Well? (Jacques uncomprehending) *Well?* (Jacques uncomprehending) What brutishness! (Jacques lowers his head) I thought I told you I was not in for anybody, except for Madame Meck.
JACQUES	Yes, Madame, but it's Madame — Madame's sister — so I thought —
MME. KRAP	My sister!
JACQUES	Yes, Madame.
MME. KRAP	You're being impertinent. (Jacques lowers his head) Show me that card. (Jacques holds out the tray again, Mme. Krap takes up the card again) Since when

	does my sister go by the name of Madame Piouk?
JACQUES	(Embarrassed) I think —
MME. KRAP	You think?
JACQUES	If Madame was to turn the card over.
	(Mme. Krap turns the card over and reads)
MME. KRAP	Couldn't you have told me so at once?
JACQUES	I beg Madame's pardon.
MME. KRAP	Don't be so humble. (Jacques silent) Think about your union.
JACQUES	Madame is joking.
MME. KRAP	Have her come in. (Jacques goes) Send in Marie.
JACQUES	Very good, Madame. (Exit)
	(Mme. Krap motionless. Enter Jacques)
	Madame Piouk.
	(Enter Madame Piouk, in great haste. Exit Jacques)
MME. PIOUK	Violette!
MME. KRAP	Marguerite!
	(They kiss)
MME. PIOUK	Violette!
MME. KRAP	You'll forgive me for not getting up. I have a slight pain in the — no matter. Sit down. I thought you were in Rome.

MME. PIOUK	(Sits down) How bad you look!
MME. KRAP	You're not so very blooming yourself.
MME. PIOUK	It's the travelling.
MME. KRAP	Who's this — (She looks at the card) — this Piouk?
MME. PIOUK	He's a doctor.
MME. KRAP	I'm not asking you what he does. (A knock) Come in. (Enter Marie) You may serve tea.
MARIE	Very good, Madame. (She goes)
MME. PIOUK	Not for me.
MME. KRAP	Marie!
MARIE	Madame?
MME. KRAP	You will serve the tea when Madame Meck is here.
MARIE	Very good, Madame. (Exit)
MME. PIOUK	You're not offering me something else?
MME. KRAP	For instance?
MME. PIOUK	A glass of port.
MME. KRAP	It's time for tea.
MME. PIOUK	How is Henri?
MME. KRAP	Poorly.
MME. PIOUK	What's wrong with him?
MME. KRAP	I don't know. He no longer urinates.
MME. PIOUK	It's the prostate.
MME. KRAP	So you got married.
MME. PIOUK	Yes.

MME. KRAP	At your age!
MME. PIOUK	We're in love.
MME. KRAP	What's the connection? (Mme. Piouk silent) But you must — I mean — you no longer must — in a word — let's see —
MME. PIOUK	Not yet.
MME. KRAP	I congratulate you.
MME. PIOUK	He wants a child.
MME. KRAP	No!
MME. PIOUK	Yes!
MME. KRAP	It's madness.
MME. PIOUK	How is Victor?
MME. KRAP	Still the same, still there, down in his hole. We never see him. (Pause) Let's not talk about it.
MME. PIOUK	You're expecting Madame Meck?
MME. KRAP	With no great impatience.
MME. PIOUK	That old witch.
MME. KRAP	You don't want to see her?
MME. PIOUK	I would just as soon not.
MME. KRAP	Yet she likes you.
MME. PIOUK	That's what you think! It's play-acting.
MME. KRAP	Yes, probably. (Pause) I expect her any minute.
MME. PIOUK	Then I'm leaving. (She gets up)
MME. KRAP	Your husband isn't with you?
MME. PIOUK	(Sitting down again) Oh I can't wait till you see him! He's so

sweet, so bright, so —

MME. KRAP	He isn't with you?
MME. PIOUK	He went to the hotel...
MME. KRAP	Which hotel?
MME. PIOUK	I don't know.
MME. KRAP	When will you know?
MME. PIOUK	He's supposed to pick me up here.
MME. KRAP	When?
MME. PIOUK	Oh in about half an hour, I think.
MME. KRAP	So you can't leave.
MME. PIOUK	I would have waited for him in the drawing room.
MME. KRAP	What kind of medicine does he do?
MME. PIOUK	He doesn't have a specialty. That is —
MME. KRAP	He does everything.
MME. PIOUK	Mankind is what interests him.
MME. KRAP	Where does he perpetrate?
MME. PIOUK	He hopes to set up a practice here.
MME. KRAP	And up until now?
MME. PIOUK	Pretty much everywhere.
MME. KRAP	I haven't congratulated you. (She puts forward her cheek which Mme. Piouk kisses) You could have let me know.
MME. PIOUK	I wanted to send you a telegram but André told me that —

MME. KRAP	Anyhow all this is of no importance. (A knock) Come in.
	(Enter Jacques)
JACQUES	Madame Meck.
	(Enter Madame Meck, a bulky woman heavily laden with furs, capes, umbrella, handbag, etc. Exit Jacques)
MME. MECK	Violette!
MME. KRAP	Jeanne! (They kiss. Mme. Meck sits down, unloads, fixes herself up) Forgive me for not getting up.
MME. MECK	You're still in pain?
MME. KRAP	Getting worse and worse. You know my sister.
MME. MECK	(Turning toward Mme. Piouk) Why it's Rose!
MME. KRAP	Of course not, it's Marguerite.
MME. MECK	My dear Marguerite! (Extends her hand, which Mme. Piouk takes) Where did you come from? I thought you were in Pisa?
MME. KRAP	She's gotten married.
MME. MECK	Married!
MME. KRAP	To a doctor who is interested in mankind.
MME. MECK	Let me give you a kiss. (Mme. Piouk lets herself be kissed) Married! Oh! — (with an undescribable movement) — I'm so glad!

MME. PIOUK	Thank you.
MME. MECK	What's his name?
MME. KRAP	(Looking at the card) Piouk, André.
MME. MECK	(Ecstatically) Madame André Piouk!
	(A knock)
MME. KRAP	Come in.
	(Enter Marie with the tea tray, which she sets down on the table)
	Has Monsieur come back?
MARIE	No, Madame.
MME. KRAP	Send Jacques in.
MARIE	Very good, Madame. (Exit)
MME. PIOUK	(To Mme. Meck) Don't you find that my sister looks bad?
MME. MECK	Bad?
	(Mme. Krap serves the tea, offers a cup to her sister who refuses)
MME. KRAP	She'd rather have port.
MME. MECK	Port! At five in the afternoon!
MME. KRAP	She's right. I'm worn out.
MME. PIOUK	What's wrong?
	(A knock)
MME. KRAP	Come in. (Enter Jacques) Ah, Jacques.
JACQUES	Madame.
MME. KRAP	Has Monsieur come back?
JACQUES	Not yet, Madame.
MME. KRAP	You will tell him, as soon as he

	does come back, that I have to speak to him.
JACQUES	Very good, Madame.
MME. KRAP	You may turn on the light.
JACQUES	Very good, Madame. (He turns on the floor lamp)
MME. KRAP	The other one too.
JACQUES	Very good, Madame. (He turns on the wall lamp)
MME. KRAP	That will be all.
JACQUES	Very good, Madame. (Exit)
MME. MECK	How is he?
MME. KRAP	Who?
MME. MECK	Henri.
MME. KRAP	Poorly.
MME. MECK	Oh.
MME. KRAP	He doesn't piss any more.
MME. MECK	Ooh!
MME. PIOUK	It's the prostate.
MME. MECK	Poor thing. And he so light-hearted, so —
MME. KRAP	What's more he is eating himself up.
MME. PIOUK	For sure.
MME. KRAP	Because of Victor.
MME. MECK	By the way, how is he?
MME. KRAP	Who?
MME. MECK	Your Victor.
MME. KRAP	Let's not talk about it.
MME. MECK	Me neither, I'm not doing well.

MME. PIOUK	What's the matter with you?
MME. MECK	It's the lower belly. It's descending, so it appears.
MME. KRAP	Like me. Except that mine has descended.
MME. PIOUK	Isn't there anything to drink in this house?
MME. KRAP	To drink?
MME. MECK	In the middle of the afternoon?
MME. PIOUK	Henri no longer pisses, Victor, we mustn't talk about it, and you, you have a descending lower belly.
MME. KRAP	And you, you've gotten married.
MME. MECK	Is that a reason to drink?
MME. KRAP	It's of no use.
MME. MECK	Our little Victor! What a thing to happen! And he so light-hearted, so alive!
MME. KRAP	He's never been either light-hearted or alive.
MME. MECK	What! Why, he was the very soul of the household, for years.
MME. KRAP	The very soul of the household! Talk about something for the books.
MME. PIOUK	He's still at the Impasse de l'Enfant-Jésus?
MME. KRAP	Jeanne sees life and light-heartedness everywhere. It's a permanent hallucination.
MME. PIOUK	He's still at the Impasse de

	l'Enfant-Jésus?
MME. KRAP	Still.
MME. PIOUK	He's got to be shaken up.
MME. KRAP	He doesn't get up any more. Another cup?
MME. MECK	Half a cup. He doesn't get up any more, you say?
MME. PIOUK	He's ill.
MME. KRAP	Nothing at all is wrong with him.
MME. MECK	Then why doesn't he get up any more?
MME. KRAP	From time to time he goes out.
MME. MECK	He gets up then from time to time.
MME. KRAP	It's when he has nothing more to eat. Then he digs around in the garbage cans. He pushes on as far as Passy. The concierge saw him.
MME. MECK	When you think of it, the garbage cans of Passy.
MME. PIOUK	It's horrible.
MME. KRAP	Isn't it though.
MME. PIOUK	But you do give him money?
MME. KRAP	Every month. I bring it to him myself.
MME. PIOUK	And what does he do with it?
MME. KRAP	How should I know? It's doubtless not enough.
	(Enter Monsieur Henri Krap)
M. KRAP	Good evening, Jeanne. Well,

	Marguerite. (They kiss) I thought you were in Venice.
MME. KRAP	Your wife is also present. (M. Krap kisses his wife) She's gotten married.
MME. MECK	To a doctor.
MME. KRAP	Who loves mankind.
M. KRAP	(Sadly) Congratulations.
MME. KRAP	Sit down.
M. KRAP	Oh, I'm not staying.
MME. KRAP	Oh, come now, of course you are.
M. KRAP	Think so? (Seats himself painfully in the armchair) I'm wrong. (Ensconces himself) I won't be able to get up again.
MME. KRAP	Don't talk nonsense.
M. KRAP	My freedom is being whittled away more and more every day. Soon I won't have the right to unlock my jaw. Me, the one who expected to make an ass of himself all the way to death's door.
MME. MECK	What's the matter with him?
MME. KRAP	He consoles himself as best he can.
M. KRAP	Yes, now I've got it, now that it's too late. *Nimis sero, imber serotinus.* Peace of mind is the hallmark of slaves. (Pause. Mme. Meck making faces) I'm the cow that, up against the bars of the slaughter-

	house, understands the utter absurdity of pastures. It would have done better to think about it earlier, out yonder, in the tall, tender grass. More's the pity. It still has the courtyard to cross. That nobody will be able to tear away from it.
MME. KRAP	Pay no attention. He thinks he's in his circle.
M. KRAP	I am. In the ninth. (Changing his tone) So, Marguerite, at last you're a respectable woman.
MME. PIOUK	Flatterer!
M. KRAP	I'm congratulating you.
MME. KRAP	You've already congratulated her.
M. KRAP	That's true.
MME. PIOUK	Henri.
M. KRAP	Yes.
MME. PIOUK	I wouldn't mind having a drink.
M. KRAP	But of course. (To Mme. Krap) The bell.
MME. KRAP	You know very well I can't get up.
M. KRAP	That's true. Besides it's not worth it. He'll come by himself.
MME. KRAP	Don't count on it. We've been left in peace now for three minutes.
M. KRAP	So, Marguerite, if you would be good enough to ring.
	(Mme. Piouk gets up, rings, sits down again)

MME. KRAP	Yesterday he stayed away a good fifteen minutes before looking in. I thought he was dead. (A knock) Come in.
	(Enter Jacques)
M. KRAP	I wonder why he always knocks. For fifteen years he's been knocking and we've been saying, Come in, and he still knocks.
MME. MECK	It's a question of correctness.
M. KRAP	(To Mme. Piouk) What will you have?
MME. PIOUK	Anything. Port.
M. KRAP	(To Jacques) Port.
JACQUES	Very good, sir. (Exit)
	(A silence)
MME. PIOUK	We were speaking about Victor.
M. KRAP	Ah.
MME. KRAP	Does there exist another subject of conversation? I begin to wonder.
MME. MECK	The poor thing!
MME. KRAP	(Violently) Be quiet!
MME. PIOUK	Violette!
MME. MECK	What's the matter with her?
MME. KRAP	The matter is that I've had enough of hearing that scoundrel being pitied and it's been going on for two years!
MME. PIOUK	Scoundrel!
MME. MECK	Your child!

M. KRAP	Two years already! Only two!
MME. KRAP	(At the height of excitation) Let him get out of the neighborhood, the city, the county, the country, let him go croak in — in the Balkans! (A knock) As for me I —
MME. PIOUK	Come in.
	(Enter Jacques)
M. KRAP	What do you want?
JACQUES	Monsieur rang?
M. KRAP	Of course not. The port.
JACQUES	At once, Monsieur. (Exit)
	(A silence)
MME. MECK	You were saying?
MME. KRAP	I wash my hands of it. (She gets up painfully) I've had enough. (Goes painfully to the door) Enough. (Exit)
MME. PIOUK	That's the way she can't get up.
MME. MECK	Where is she going?
M. KRAP	(With a sigh) To the toilet probably. She goes there from time to time.
	(A silence)
MME. MECK	You look marvellous.
MME. PIOUK	She isn't serious.
MME. MECK	What?
MME. PIOUK	Violette. They're idle words.
MME. MECK	Of course. Washing her hands of him! Her only child! Can you

	imagine!
	(A knock)
M. KRAP	(Too low) Come in.
MME. MECK	A mother doing that!
	(Another knock)
MME. PIOUK	Come in! (Enter Jacques carrying a tray. He looks for a place to put it) Place it on the chair. (He places the tray on Mme. Krap's chair) On the other one. (He places it on the other chair) You will ask Marie to come and clear the table.
JACQUES	Very good, Madame. (Exit)
MME. PIOUK	When one has servants one is no longer in one's own home.
MME. MECK	They're needed all the same.
	(A silence)
MME. PIOUK	I've been without news for so long. So is there something new in this business?
M. KRAP	What business?
MME. PIOUK	This business of Victor.
M. KRAP	Not one new item.
MME. MECK	It appears that he comes as far as Rue Spontini to dig around in the garbage cans.
M. KRAP	I wasn't told anything.
MME. PIOUK	You don't seem to care a bit.
M. KRAP	You mean that?
MME. MECK	I never understood a thing about

	this business.
M. KRAP	Dramatically speaking, my wife's absence serves no purpose.
	(Mesdames Piouk and Meck exchange looks. A knock)
MME. PIOUK	Oh, come in!
	(Enter Marie. Tray business. Exit Marie)
	Do you want some?
MME. MECK	A drop.
MME. PIOUK	And you, Henri?
M. KRAP	Thank you, no.
	(Mme. Piouk serves Mme. Meck)
MME. MECK	Oh that's too much! I'll be tipsy! (She drinks) It's strong!
	(Mme. Piouk serves herself, empties her glass in one gulp, pours herself a second) She's been long.
MME. PIOUK	What?
MME. MECK	Violette has been long.
M. KRAP	You think so?
MME. PIOUK	But something must be done! He can't be left like that.
M. KRAP	Like what?
MME. PIOUK	In that — that sordid inertia.
M. KRAP	And if it's what he wants.
MME. PIOUK	But it's a disgrace to the family!
MME. MECK	It's not right at his age.
MME. PIOUK	It will kill Violette.

M. KRAP	You don't know her.
	(A silence)
MME. PIOUK	(To Mme. Meck) How is the general? (A silence) Or should I say field-marshal?
	(Handkerchief of Mme. Meck)
M. KRAP	Come now, Marguerite, think about what you're saying.
MME. PIOUK	I don't understand.
M. KRAP	There's a shade of difference between mourning-wear and chic.
MME. PIOUK	Oh, poor Jeanne, I didn't know, I'm dreadfully sorry, forgive me, forgive me.
MME. MECK	(Drawing upon the military tradition) His last breath was for France.
	(A knock)
MME. PIOUK	That is becoming impossible.
M. KRAP	We would be better off leaving the door open. Or roundly doing away with it.
	(Another knock)
MME. PIOUK	So just come in for crying out loud!
	(Enter Jacques)
JACQUES	Doctor Piouk.
M. KRAP	Don't know him.
MME. PIOUK	André! (Rushes out)
M. KRAP	Who?

Mme. Meck	Her husband.
M. Krap	(To Jacques) Have you seen Madame?
Jacques	Madame has gone out, Monsieur.
M. Krap	Gone out!
Jacques	Yes, Monsieur.
M. Krap	On foot?
Jacques	Yes, Monsieur.
M. Krap	She didn't say where she was going?
Jacques	Madame didn't say anything, Monsieur.
M. Krap	That will do.
	(Exit Jacques)
Mme. Meck	*Vive la France!* Then came the coma.
M. Krap	I beg your pardon?
Mme. Meck	I was reliving Ludovic's last moments.
M. Krap	And then what?
Mme. Meck	Raising himself roughly into a sitting position, he cried out, *Vive la France!* Then he fell back and went into his death rattle.
M. Krap	He was able to raise himself into a sitting position?
Mme. Meck	Yes, to the great amazement of every one of us. (Enter Madame and Dr. Piouk. He is a hideously ugly man. Embarrassed silence. Introductions. Dr. Piouk sits

down)

MME. PIOUK	A bit of port, my darling?
DR. PIOUK	Thank you.
MME. PIOUK	Thank you yes or no thank you?
DR. PIOUK	No thank you.
M. KRAP	You'll excuse me for not getting up. I have a slight pain in the — I'm tired.
DR. PIOUK	You are suffering?
M. KRAP	Dying.
MME. MECK	Come, come, Henri, calm down.
M. KRAP	And I have every intention of amazing nobody.
MME. MECK	Henri!
M. KRAP	By raising myself into a sitting position.
MME. PIOUK	Where is Violette?
M. KRAP	My unbefitting position. Ha! Ha!
DR. PIOUK	A little port, after all.
	(Mme. Piouk serves him)
MME. MECK	She went out.
M. KRAP	What?
MME. MECK	Marguerite is asking where Violette is. I am telling her she went out.
MME. PIOUK	(Decanter in hand) Went out!
M. KRAP	On foot.
MME. MECK	Without saying where she was going.
M. KRAP	She won't be long getting back.

MME. PIOUK	She told you?
M. KRAP	She's never long getting back.
MME. MECK	May what you say be the truth.
M. KRAP	Why?
MME. MECK	I'll be able to leave with an easy mind.
M. KRAP	My son's way is the truth.
MME. PIOUK	Henri!
M. KRAP	I'm cutting loose.
MME. MECK	(Pursuing her train of thought) Without seeing her in my mind's eye, all bloody, run over by a truck.
M. KRAP	It's she who runs over the trucks.
DR. PIOUK	(Getting up) My darling —
M. KRAP	My darling, my darling.
DR. PIOUK	It is time we left.
M. KRAP	Jeanne.
MME. MECK	Henri.
M. KRAP	You remember the early days of my marriage to Violette?
MME. MECK	Do I remember!
M. KRAP	Before we'd learned to appreciate each other.
MME. MECK	Those were the good old days.
M. KRAP	Did I have occasion to say darling to her?
MME. MECK	You used to coo.
M. KRAP	I can't imagine.
DR. PIOUK	(Still standing) Marguerite.

MME. PIOUK	I'm coming, darling.
M. KRAP	My wife will be so sorry. Terribly so.
MME. MECK	Me too, I should also be going.
M. KRAP	But you're staying.
MME. MECK	That is —
M. KRAP	You see, the world outside is calling to her, but she makes a point of holding out. But Marguerite has never been led by anything but her own inclinations. I'm not saying this for your benefit, Doctor.
MME. PIOUK	You're being ungracious, Henri.
M. KRAP	(Without warmth) Stay for dinner, we're having cold cuts.
DR. PIOUK	Most kind. Unfortunately we are expected elsewhere.
M. KRAP	(To Mme. Meck, lewdly) Aren't they in a hurry!
MME. MECK	Be patient just five more minutes.
M. KRAP	Come come, a little restraint.
MME. MECK	I will bring you back. In the Delage.
DR. PIOUK	How about it, Marguerite?
MME. PIOUK	Whatever you like, my darling.
M. KRAP	The longer you wait, the better it is.
MME. PIOUK	I would so have liked you — Violette to get to know you.
	(Dr. Piouk sits down again. A

	silence)
M. KRAP	*Vous prenez un cigare?*
DR. PIOUK	Thank you.
M. KRAP	Thank you yes or no thank you?
DR. PIOUK	I don't smoke.
	(A silence)
MME. MECK ⎫ MME. PIOUK ⎭	(Together) I —
MME. MECK	Oh, sorry. You were saying?
MME. PIOUK	Oh, nothing. Go on.
	(A silence)
M. KRAP	Well, Jeanne, spit it out.
MME. MECK	(Upon reflection) My goodness, I don't know any more.
	(A silence)
M. KRAP	Incapable of reflection myself, it is my organs that have taken over. (A silence) It is with you, Doctor, that I am striving to open communication.
DR. PIOUK	Oh, you know, I'm not much of a talker.
MME. PIOUK	He thinks so much!
M. KRAP	Nonetheless, what I've just said isn't devoid of intelligence.
DR. PIOUK	It is meaningless.
M. KRAP	Wait a minute! Meaning what?
DR. PIOUK	You are your organs, Monsieur, and your organs are you.

M. KRAP	I am my organs?
DR. PIOUK	That is so.
M. KRAP	You are frightening me.
MME. MECK	(Sniffing out free medical advice) And me, Doctor, am I also my organs?
DR. PIOUK	Without the least bit left over, Madame.
M. KRAP	What a pleasure to meet at last an intelligent man!
MME. PIOUK	(Ecstatically) André!
M. KRAP	Please do go on. Elaborate on this grandiose train of thought.
DR. PIOUK	This isn't the right time.
M. KRAP	Before the return of that heap of obsolete organs known as my wife.
MME. PIOUK	Henri!
DR. PIOUK	Please.
M. KRAP	You're going to force me to visit your office.
	(A knock)
MME. PIOUK	Come in.
	(Enter Jacques)
JACQUES	Mademoiselle Skunk.
	(Enter Mademoiselle Skunk, an alluring young lady. Greetings, hers glum. Exit Jacques)
MME. PIOUK	You remember me?
MLLE. SKUNK	Of course.
MME. PIOUK	It was two years ago, at Evian.

MLLE. SKUNK	What was I doing there? (A silence)
MME. PIOUK	May I introduce you to my husband, Doctor Piouk. (Mlle. Skunk sits down in Mme. Krap's seat)
MME. MECK	You look marvellous.
MME. PIOUK	A bit of port?
MLLE. SKUNK	If you like.
M. KRAP	Doctor.
DR. PIOUK	(Torn from his thoughts, makes a show of giving a start) Did someone call my name?
M. KRAP	I'm wondering of what use you're going to be in this farce.
DR. PIOUK	(Upon mature reflection) I hope that I will be able to be useful.
MME. MECK	(Worried) I don't understand.
DR. PIOUK	And your role, my dear sir, is it very clear-cut?
M. KRAP	It is being cut.
DR. PIOUK	Yet you are on stage.
M. KRAP	So it appears.
MME. MECK	I absolutely must go.
M. KRAP	Go, my dear Jeanne, go, since go you absolutely must. We don't need you.
MLLE. SKUNK	Where is Violette?
DR. PIOUK	(To M. Krap) Forcing things a bit you might perhaps manage to

amuse the rubbernecks.

M. KRAP	You think so? From the bottom of your heart?
DR. PIOUK	I say it as I think it.
M. KRAP	That is a possibility I hadn't caught sight of.
MLLE. SKUNK	Where is Violette?
MME. MECK	It is a getting worrisome.
M. KRAP	What are you saying?
MME. MECK	Olga is asking where Violette is and I am saying it is getting worrisome.
M. KRAP	What is getting worrisome?
MME. MECK	This inordinate absence.
M. KRAP	Inordinate absence! Only Jeanne comes up with words like that.
MLLE. SKUNK	Where did she go?
MME. MECK	That we do not know.
M. KRAP	Driven by who knows what she left the house on a sudden impulse, on foot. For the longest time we thought she was in the toilet. That's it, right, Doctor?
DR. PIOUK	Intricate to a fault. Keep at it.
MLLE. SKUNK	She asked me to come by before dinner.
M. KRAP	She had to speak to you?
MLLE. SKUNK	Yes, about things that couldn't wait.
M. KRAP	She had to speak to me as well, so it appears. In fact it is the only

	reason why I am here among you, as you can easily imagine. And yet she still hasn't told me anything.
MME. MECK	(To Mlle. Skunk) Have you seen Victor?
M. KRAP	Right now I'm the one who goes to speak to him.
MLLE. SKUNK	Last week.
M. KRAP	(To Dr. Piouk) Mlle. Skunk is my son's fiancée.
DR. PIOUK	Fortunate young man.
MLLE. SKUNK	(Bitterly) He cannot contain himself for joy.
	(Dr. Piouk lights a cigarette)
M. KRAP	I thought you didn't smoke.
DR. PIOUK	I lied to you.
MME. MECK	I am going to have to leave.
M. KRAP	You're not going to start in again.
MME. MECK	What's to be done?
M. KRAP	The time one wastes with such people. Go. We will call you.
MLLE. SKUNK	I am going with you.
	(A fierce-sounding voice is heard)
M. KRAP	Peekaboo, there she is.
MME. MECK	At last!
DR. PIOUK	(To Mlle. Skunk) You're French, Mademoiselle?
MLLE. SKUNK	No, Monsieur.
MME. MECK	You are sure that it's her?
M. KRAP	I am convinced of it.

DR. PIOUK	Scandinavian?
	(A knock)
MME. PIOUK	Come in.
	(Enter Jacques)
JACQUES	Madame is asking for Monsieur.
M. KRAP	It sounds like a classified ad.
MME. MECK	There isn't anything the matter with Madame?
M. KRAP	You will tell Madame that — (Changes his mind). Help resuscitate me. (Jacques rushes over, helps M. Krap to get up, wants to hold him up as far as the door. M. Krap motions to him to get out of the way. Reaching the door he turns around) You see! Once I'm up I walk all by myself! I go out! (Exit. He comes back in) I come back in! And I go back out! (Exit, followed by Jacques)
MME. PIOUK	Henri is very much changed.
DR. PIOUK	Don't tell me you are English.
MME. MECK	Believing he is doomed, he no longer restrains himself.
MME. PIOUK	That's convenient.
DR. PIOUK	(Disheartened) He's a remarkable man.
MME. PIOUK	You really think so?
DR. PIOUK	I say it as I think it.
MME. PIOUK	But from what viewpoint?
DR. PIOUK	That is difficult to say.

MME. PIOUK	Indeed this is the first time I am hearing it.
DR. PIOUK	What does he do?
MME. MECK	(With pride) He is a man of letters.
DR. PIOUK	You don't say!
	(Enter M. Krap. He reaches his armchair and cautiously sits down)
M. KRAP	You were saying nice things about me, I feel it.
MME. MECK	There isn't anything the matter with her?
M. KRAP	She is unharmed.
MME. MECK	She is coming?
M. KRAP	She's getting ready for that.
MME. PIOUK	There was a time when you were unaffected.
M. KRAP	At the cost of what artifice!
DR. PIOUK	You are a writer, Monsieur?
M. KRAP	(Indignant) What gives you leave to —
DR. PIOUK	It can be felt in the way you express yourself.
MME. PIOUK	Where has she been?
MME. MECK	She is going to tell us.
M. KRAP	I will be frank with you. I *was* a writer.
MME. MECK	He is a member of the Institute!
M. KRAP	What did I tell you.

DR. PIOUK	What genre?
M. KRAP	I don't follow you.
DR. PIOUK	I speak of your writings. Your preferences were for what genre?
M. KRAP	For the shit genre.
MME. PIOUK	Really.
DR. PIOUK	Prose or poetry?
M. KRAP	One day the former, another day the latter.
DR. PIOUK	And you now deem your body of work to be complete?
M. KRAP	The Lord has flushed me out.
DR. PIOUK	A small book of memoirs does not tempt you?
M. KRAP	That would spoil the death throes.
MME. MECK	Admit that this is a bizarre way to treat one's guests.
MLLE. SKUNK	Extremely odd.
M. KRAP	Marguerite, would you mind changing places with Olga?
MME. PIOUK	I am happy where I am.
M. KRAP	I know. We are all happy where we are. Very, very happy. Unfortunately our happiness is not the issue.
Mme. Meck	Which new freak is this?
M. KRAP	Don't you see, Marguerite, since you do need to be told everything, whether we see you or whether we don't see you is so to speak of no importance. I for one would not

see the slightest drawback in your disappearing this very minute. Olga, on the other hand, has a place among us only in so far as she shows off her charms, that is to say her breasts and her legs, for her face is rather commonplace.

MME. PIOUK   As a boor you are moving ahead.

M. KRAP   Marguerite, you are wrong to take offense. As a brother-in-law I'm fond of you, very fond, and I would be absolutely heartbroken to see you move away. But as a — how can I put it — (He snaps his fingers).

DR. PIOUK   Hierophant.

M. KRAP   If you like.

(A silence)

DR. PIOUK   So, finish your phrase.

M. KRAP   What was I saying?

DR. PIOUK   As a brother-in-law you are fond of her, as a hierophant you — ?

M. KRAP   (His voice breaking) I have no family.

MME. PIOUK   He is crying!

DR. PIOUK   Do as he asks, Marguerite.

(Mme. Piouk and Mlle. Skunk change places)

M. KRAP   (To Mlle. Skunk) Open up your jacket. Cross your legs. Lift your skirt. (He helps her) There. Don't budge one inch.

DR. PIOUK   This is what we call a momentary
lapse.

M. KRAP   I am subject to a fair number of
them.

MME. MECK   (Exploding) I have had enough!

M. KRAP   We have all had enough. But that
is not the issue.

MME. MECK   For me it is the issue. (Rises
massively and gathers her numer-
ous belongings. Digs around in
her enormous bag, finally brings
out a card and reads) *I must see
you. Come have tea tomorrow. I have a
million things to tell you. We will be
alone.* (She allows time for the
message to have its effect) I don't
like to have my leg pulled.

M. KRAP   People are truly unbelievable.

DR. PIOUK   It is human nature.

M. KRAP   The minute they believe they are
not having their leg pulled, they
put up with everything.

DR. PIOUK   We are put together just that way.

M. KRAP   Poor Jeanne, you might just as
well stay seated as beat around the
bush standing up, giving way
under the weight of your equip-
ment. She commands the stage,
by God, and it hasn't got a thing
to do with her!

MME. MECK   (In the tone of a pythoness) I am

but an old woman, ugly, ill and
alone. Yet the day will come when
all of you envy me.

(A silence)

M. KRAP   Touché.

(Exit Mme. Meck, slamming the
door)

DR. PIOUK   She has great foresight.

M. KRAP   But whom don't we envy?

DR. PIOUK   She perhaps has a function you
don't suspect.

M. KRAP   Doctor, you are getting caught up
in the game! Watch out!

DR. PIOUK   I won't deny its charm.

MLLE. SKUNK   (Yawning deeply) Sorry!

MME. PIOUK   But this light is horrible!

MLLE. SKUNK   You are no longer under it
though.

MME. PIOUK   Now I see it.

MLLE. SKUNK   What is this wire for?

(She points to a thin strip of
barbed wire which, held in place
beneath the edge of the table,
extends down to the floor)

MME. PIOUK   Wire?

MLLE. SKUNK   (Putting her hand on it) It has
sharp points! Look.

(Mme. Piouk gets up and leans
forward over the table)

MME. PIOUK   How is it that I didn't notice it?

DR. PIOUK	My wife is but barely attuned to the macrocosm.
M. KRAP	Yet she did react to the lighting.
DR. PIOUK	It's that it really made her suffer.
MLLE. SKUNK	But what is the meaning of that?
M. KRAP	It is Victor's seat.
DR. PIOUK	He is your son?
M. KRAP	Yes, I am sure of it now.
DR. PIOUK	He took up a lot of space?
M. KRAP	Yes, he took hold of a lot of space, in this house.
MLLE. SKUNK	I don't understand.
M. KRAP	What don't you understand, my little Olga?
MLLE. SKUNK	What that (She points to the wire) has to do with Victor.
M. KRAP	Everything has to be explained to them.
DR. PIOUK	There you have woman.
M. KRAP	Don't you see, my little Olga, since Victor's departure, about two years ago, I believe —
MLLE. SKUNK	Two years! Two years five months!
M. KRAP	What is important about that?
MLLE. SKUNK	For heaven's sake!
M. KRAP	Shall I go on? (A silence) Since that — er — that event, my wife has always had the desire to preserve, while so to speak doing away with, the spots favored by our son, for all of us had our

favorite spots in this house, Victor, my wife and I, going as far back as I can remember, and speaking for myself personally I am still holding on to mine. (Pause) My wife threw herself into this project — long postponed, why I don't know — last week, and the results lie here before you. And it is only a beginning. Soon the apartment will be full of barbed wire. (Pause) It must be said, in Violette's defense, that for one whole afternoon she was under the spell of the Surrealist Exhibition. (Pause) Is this sufficiently clear?

DR. PIOUK	Much too clear. You have botched everything.
M. KRAP	Doctor, you disappoint me.
DR. PIOUK	Are you insinuating that I've said something stupid?
MME. PIOUK	He is insane.
M. KRAP	Immensely stupid, Doctor. For one must smile at one's own smile.
DR. PIOUK	You are right, Marguerite. (Enter Madame Krap)
M. KRAP	Enter the Rock of Gibraltar.
MME. PIOUK	André, this is my sister. Violette, I — (Dr. Piouk gets up)
M. KRAP	I am sorry for not getting up. I

	have a slight pain in the —
MME. KRAP	Marguerite, you have taken my seat.
MME. PIOUK	(Rising hastily) Take it.
	(Mme. Krap sits down in her seat, Mme. Piouk sits down in that of Mme. Meck)
MME. KRAP	Good evening, Olga.
MLLE. SKUNK	Good evening. You wanted to see me?
MME. KRAP	Yes. Who is this man?
MME. PIOUK	He is my husband. (She gets up) Coming, André?
MME. KRAP	(Forcefully) Sit down!
	(Mme. Piouk wavers)
M. KRAP	Be careful.
	(Mme. Piouk sits down again)
MME. KRAP	Doctor — let's see —
DR. PIOUK	Piouk. (He bows and sits down again)
MME. KRAP	Marguerite has told us that you love mankind. Is that possible?
MME. PIOUK	You distort my words.
DR. PIOUK	I do not love it.
MME. PIOUK	It interests him. Period.
MME. KRAP	You are interested in mankind?
DR. PIOUK	It has its moments.
MME. KRAP	You are not a Communist?
DR. PIOUK	My private life is my own business.
M. KRAP	Doctor, don't make things worse.

MME. PIOUK	Where have you been? We were beginning to worry. André did not want to wait. But when I told him how much you wanted to meet him —
MME. KRAP	It is a sticky problem.
DR. PIOUK	Which one?
MME. KRAP	That of mankind.
DR. PIOUK	Off hand, I would agree.
M. KRAP	The best thinkers have wrestled with it.
DR. PIOUK	I do not pretend to have surpassed them.
MME. KRAP	And what is your solution?
DR. PIOUK	My solution?
M. KRAP	In a word.
MME. KRAP	(Sternly) You do have one, I hope.
DR. PIOUK	It lacks charm.
M. KRAP	That can't be helped.
DR. PIOUK	Is this really the right time?
M. KRAP	It is certainly the first time I have heard someone being pleaded with —
MME. KRAP	Be quiet!
M. KRAP	To clear up the situation of the human race.
DR. PIOUK	It does not seem to be the right moment.
MME. KRAP	We will be the judge of that.

M. Krap	Do your duty.
Dr. Piouk	So, here is what I would do —
M. Krap	There are things to *do*?
Dr. Piouk	I am a practical soul.
Mme. Krap	Would you be quiet?
M. Krap	Yes, Violette, I would indeed.
Mme. Krap	We are listening.
Dr. Piouk	Here it is. I would prohibit reproduction. I would perfect the condom and other appliances and generalize their use. I would create state-run corps of abortionists. I would impose the death sentence on every woman guilty of having given birth. I would drown the newborn. I would campaign in favor of homosexuality and myself set the example. And to get things going, I would encourage by every means the recourse to euthanasia, without, however, making it an obligation. Here you have the broad outlines.
Mme. Krap	I was born too soon.
M. Krap	Much too soon.
Dr. Piouk	I do not lay claim to originality. It is a matter of organization. There is where I have opened up new horizons. In two years everything will be in position. Unfortunately, my strength is ebbing. My inner resources as well.

MME. KRAP	And that child you want?
DR. PIOUK	Who told you that I want a child? (A silence)
MME. PIOUK	(To Mme. Krap) You are hateful.
MME. KRAP	Doctor, you will kill her.
DR. PIOUK	I want a child, first off, to amuse me during my leisure hours, more and more brief and dreary; second, that it should receive the torch from my hands, when they can no longer bear it.
M. KRAP	That in essence is the advantage of sons.
MME. KRAP	But you will kill her.
DR. PIOUK	For a long time I have been debating this very question with your sister, Madame, quite as much before as since we were united. Isn't that so, Marguerite?
MME. PIOUK	You were just perfect.
Dr. Piouk	During those delightful, awful weeks preceding our vows, while we roamed hand in hand in the Campagna or, on the terraces of Tivoli, sought the advice of the moon, our conversation ran almost entirely on this very question. Isn't that so, Marguerite?
MME. PIOUK	Almost solely, my darling.
MME. KRAP	(To M. Krap) What's the matter with you, there, sneering away in

your corner?

| M. KRAP | I was thinking about the moon and you and me, seeking its advice. |

| DR. PIOUK | Engaged at last, we went though hideous periods and, speaking for myself, I would not want to relive them, not for anything. |

| M. KRAP | What can you do? Engaged humans are that way. I recall a certain night, in Robinson. Violette was ahead of me in the tree and I assure you — |

| MME. KRAP | Be quiet! |

| DR. PIOUK | And since our official, open cohabitation which, by the way, was blessed by His Holiness, how many nights have we not worn out, until cock crow, weighing the pros and cons, incapable of making a decision? |

| M. KRAP | You should have taken the plunge head first. |

| DR. PIOUK | That is what we did — (He takes out his memorandum-book and flips through it) — wait — on the Saturday night preceding Sunday last. (He turns a few pages, makes a note of something, puts the memorandum-book back in his pocket) And you see, we were sick and tired of splitting hairs. (Ex- |

	pressive gesture) Now we are waiting. (He gets up) And by the will of God.
MME. KRAP	What is the matter with you?
DR. PIOUK	The matter with me?
MME. KRAP	You are not going to leave us?
M. KRAP	I invited them for dinner. But they are all fired up to be alone.
MME. KRAP	To stay for dinner! Using what?
M. KRAP	I don't know. Yesterday's lamb.
MME. KRAP	Lamb! You mean mutton. What am I saying, mutton, ram, it smells of wool and coupling all over the house.
DR. PIOUK	You tempt me. Unfortunately we are expected somewhere.
M. KRAP	Put yourself in their place.
MME. KRAP	If I were fifty, no, that's too much, forty years younger, Doctor, I would go with you to all the hot spots, in spite of the fact that strictly speaking you do not make much of an impression on me. But when you speak...! (To M. Krap) What are you saying?
M. KRAP	Nothing. I was quivering.
MME. PIOUK	We are expected somewhere.
DR. PIOUK	Now let's not get carried away, dearest.
MME. KRAP	Let's go to the Terminus.
DR. PIOUK	Mlle. Skunk is not saying any-

	thing.
MLLE. SKUNK	What do you want me to say? I am waiting to know why I was summoned.
MME. KRAP	You will come with us. We'll all get drunk.
DR. PIOUK	I just love blowouts.
M. KRAP	And your lower belly?
MME. KRAP	I will speak to the Doctor about it. Would you be so kind, Doctor?
DR. PIOUK	Not before the cheese, dear lady.
MME. KRAP	Look here, you rascal you!
MME. PIOUK	(To Mme. Krap) Your outing did you a world of good.
	(A silence)
DR. PIOUK	You will come, Mademoiselle?
MLLE. SKUNK	I am free.
MME. KRAP	It's decided. The Terminus, in half an hour.
	(Everybody gets up, except M. Krap and Mlle. Skunk)
DR. PIOUK	(To M. Krap) See you soon. I have many things to tell you.
M. KRAP	Forgive me for not getting up, I have a slight —
MME. KRAP	I will show you out. Aren't you coming, Olga?
MLLE. SKUNK	I will go with you. I don't feel like changing.
DR. PIOUK	(To Mlle. Skunk) Now don't let us down!

MME. KRAP	(To Mlle. Skunk) As you like. (Exit Mme. Krap, Mme. and Dr. Piouk. A rather long silence)
M. KRAP	Open your jacket.
MLLE. SKUNK	I am cold.
M. KRAP	That does not matter. Lift up your skirt. Again. There. Now keep still. Breathe in. (Mlle. Skunk takes her head in her hands, bends all the way over and weeps. She is shaken with sobs) God damn it! (The fit goes on) Stop! (Mlle. Skunk is sobbing worse than ever) She cries like a scullion. (He raises his voice) You are ugly, Olga, you hear me, disgustingly ugly. We're done for. (Mlle. Skunk calms down little by little, lifts up her worn-looking face, crosses her legs which grief had uncrossed, lifts up her skirt, etc.) You are pretty! Who taught you to blubber as if — (He is loath to repeat himself) — as if — (It does not come to him) — as in life? You are forgetting where you are.
MLLE. SKUNK	You know very well.
M. KRAP	What?
MLLE. SKUNK	Who taught me.
M. KRAP	That is not the question. And what about me, you think I don't feel like howling? Only in my case,

if I — (He stops himself, struck by a horrible suspicion) You never carried on like that in front of him needless to say?

MLLE. SKUNK	Of course not.
M. KRAP	You swear it?
MLLE. SKUNK	Yes.
M. KRAP	Then all is still not lost.
MLLE. SKUNK	I dare say I should have.
M. KRAP	What?
MLLE. SKUNK	Wept in front of him, as in life. (A silence)
M. KRAP	That would have gotten you nowhere.
MLLE. SKUNK	Maybe it would have. (A silence)
M. KRAP	I'm not much longer for this world.
MLLE. SKUNK	You mustn't say that.
M. KRAP	I feel like getting it off my chest. (Pause) For once. (Pause) With someone who does not hate me. (Pause) But maybe you do hate me.
MLLE. SKUNK	You know very well I don't.
M. KRAP	Why?
MLLE. SKUNK	I don't know.
M. KRAP	It is a thing I believe I have known only lately. (A silence) Are you willing?
MLLE. SKUNK	I am such a blockhead.

M. KRAP	What does it matter?
MLLE. SKUNK	I will not understand.
M. KRAP	You will think about it now and then?
MLLE. SKUNK	Yes, of course, father.
M. KRAP	Father?
MLLE. SKUNK	What? (Pause) I called you father?
M. KRAP	It did seem so.
MLLE. SKUNK	(Embarrassed) Oh! (Her lips tremble)
M. KRAP	Don't start in again. (Mlle. Skunk gets a grip on herself) You will weep when you are alone.
MLLE. SKUNK	Yes. (A silence)
M. KRAP	Don't leave your post. I am searching for my ideas. They are scattered. As on a battlefield. (Pause) Attention. I am going to begin.
MLLE. SKUNK	Don't go too fast.
M. KRAP	(In a doctrinal tone) The error is one of wanting to live. It is not possible. There is nothing to live off, in the life that is lent us. How stupid it all is!
MLLE. SKUNK	Yes.
M. KRAP	Am I not right? I resume. It is a question of materials. Either there are too many and you do not know where to begin or there are too few and it is not worth your

while to begin. But all the same you do begin, afraid of doing nothing. Sometimes you even believe you are going to finish, that does happen. Then you see it is only a bluff. So you begin again, within the too much and the too little. Why can't you make the best of a life that is only a bluff? It must be the divine origin. They tell you life is just that, beginning and beginning again. Not so, it is only the fear of doing nothing. Life is not possible. I am not putting it right.

MLLE. SKUNK   I do not understand anything.

M. KRAP   That imbecile of a doctor, with his abortions and his euthanasia. Did you hear him?

MLLE. SKUNK   I did not pay very much attention.

M. KRAP   A technician of the basest sort.

MLLE. SKUNK   I do not know what you mean when you speak of life and of living. Victor neither, I do not understand him at all. I am one who feels myself living. Why do you want that to have a meaning?

M. KRAP   My God! wind it up and it also thinks.

MLLE. SKUNK   You cannot say quite simply what you want?

M. KRAP   What I would have wanted?

MLLE. SKUNK	If you prefer.
M. KRAP	I would have wanted to be pleased, for a whole moment.
MLLE. SKUNK	But pleased with *what?*
M. KRAP	With having been born, and with not yet having died. (A silence) I am finishing up quickly, for I have a feeling my wife draws near.
MLLE. SKUNK	The end of life?
M. KRAP	My WIFE. That catastrophe.
MLLE. SKUNK	But —
M. KRAP	One moment. Finding it therefore impossible to live and recoiling from the great cure, through a sense of decency, or through cowardice, or because of the very fact that he is not living, what can man do to avoid the oh so very discreet and unobtrusive insanity he has been taught to dread? (Pause) He can pretend to be living and that others live. (Raises his hand) One moment. That is the solution, the ruse rather, I have been rallying round these many days. I do not say that it is the only one. But I am too old to be learning from my — no, I will mention no names. And there you have it. No, do not ask me any questions, for I cannot answer them. You are smiling, but that

	doesn't matter. You should smile more often. Except when you feel like it. Like me. (He unlocks his jaw in an enormous frozen smile. Mlle. Skunk recoils. End of smile)
MLLE. SKUNK	You are horrid.
M. KRAP	Yes. And another thing.
MLLE. SKUNK	No, no, I have had enough.
M. KRAP	I ask only that you say yes.
MLLE. SKUNK	Say yes? To what?
M. KRAP	To a little prayer.
MLLE. SKUNK	No, no, I cannot.
M. KRAP	Promise. I am dying. (A silence) You will pretend to live for my son's sake.
MLLE. SKUNK	Yes, yes, anything you want.
M. KRAP	So that he looks like he is living.
MLLE. SKUNK	Yes, yes, I promise.
M. KRAP	You have missed the point.
MLLE. SKUNK	I promise, I promise. (A silence)
M. KRAP	You have no desire to kiss me. (Mlle. Skunk starts to cry again) It doesn't matter. You are right. And please do not start crying. Wait — (Enter Mme. Krap) wait until you are alone.
MME. KRAP	You are ready, Olga?
MLLE. SKUNK	At once. (She gets up, goes)
MME. KRAP	Where are you going?
MLLE. SKUNK	To freshen up. (Exit)

M. Krap	She understood.
Mme. Krap	Hurry up, Victor.
M. Krap	Victor? My name is not Victor.
Mme. Krap	Hurry up. You haven't even shaved.
M. Krap	I am not going out.
Mme. Krap	(Taking him by the arm) Out you go, get up.
M. Krap	Do not make me have to kill you, Violette.
Mme. Krap	Kill me! You! Kill me! Me! (Laughs heartily)
M. Krap	(Taking a razor out of his pocket) Help me get up. (Mme. Krap draws back) I would have pre-ferred (He tries to get up) to leave you to your cancer. More's the pity. (He half-rises)
Mme. Krap	(Moving back toward the door) You are completely mad!
M. Krap	(Still floundering around in his armchair) Once I'm up it will be plain sailing.
Mme. Krap	(Realizing he cannot get up) You stinking old cripple! (Comes back toward him) To think that you frightened me even for a minute!
M. Krap	(Dropping back again) Not easy to sit up straight, even to kill your wife.
Mme. Krap	Scoundrel!

M. KRAP	Me too?
MME. KRAP	Scum!
M. KRAP	In any case, you'll get what you deserve. I will cut your throat tonight, while you are snoring away.
MME. KRAP	(Terror-stricken at the prospects thus opened up and perhaps in particular by that of spending an anxious evening among her guests) Henri, don't be like that. Come to your senses! Think of all we have gone through together! To our great sorrow! Let us be friends.
M. KRAP	(Graciously) Sit down for a minute or two. (Mme. Krap sits down) You saw Victor?
MME. KRAP	I swear that I did not. I have simply been walking. I was irritated. I have already told you that.
M. KRAP	What did he say to you? (Enter Mlle. Skunk)
MME. KRAP	Wait for me one minute, Olga. I am coming immediately. (Exit Mlle. Skunk)
M. KRAP	There is no need to admit that you are lying, nor to apologize for it. Simply tell me what he said to you.
MME. KRAP	(Straining) He told me that he did not want to see me any more.

M. KRAP	And you, how were you?
MME. KRAP	How was I? I do not understand.
M. KRAP	You played the worried mother.
MME. KRAP	I am terribly worried.
M. KRAP	Then threatening. Then tearful. (A silence) For the five-hundredth time. (A silence) You implored, shouted, cried. (A silence. Violently) Answer!
MME. KRAP	But of course, Henri, you're well aware of that.
M. KRAP	(Reassured) Excellent. (Mme. Krap gets up) Just a moment. (Mme. Krap sits down again) You threatened to cut him off?
MME. KRAP	Yes, I told him that this could no longer go on.
M. KRAP	Will wonders never cease.
MME. KRAP	I had already warned him of it.
M. KRAP	But without pushing him to the wall?
MME. KRAP	Yes.
M. KRAP	It is today that you were to bring him the money?
MME. KRAP	Yes.
M. KRAP	Then why did you invite Jeanne?
MME. KRAP	I wanted her to come with me.
M. KRAP	Then Marguerite came?
MME. KRAP	Yes.
M. KRAP	You saw Jeanne before she left?

MME. KRAP	Yes.
M. KRAP	You said nothing to her?
MME. KRAP	No. She was furious.
M. KRAP	You gave it to him?
MME. KRAP	What?
M. KRAP	You gave him the money?
MME. KRAP	No.
M. KRAP	What did he say?
MME. KRAP	That it was of no importance.
M. KRAP	And that he did not want to see you anymore?
MME. KRAP	Yes.
M. KRAP	Fine fine fine. (He rubs his hands. Mme. Krap weeps. Handkerchief. She controls herself) Oh! you've already finished?
MME. KRAP	One must not give way.
M. KRAP	Yes, do! do! on the contrary, it is — (He breaks off, struck by a painful thought) But what are you going to do right now?
MME. KRAP	What I am going to do?
M. KRAP	You are not going over there any more?
MME. KRAP	I don't know.
M. KRAP	But you have no more tricks up your sleeve. (An interval) Unless you find something else.
MME. KRAP	For sure we will find something. It cannot go on like this.

M. Krap	Bravo!
Mme. Krap	Can it?
M. Krap	Why, of course not. For sure we will find something. (Mme. Krap gets up) So that it does go on like this.
Mme. Krap	What?
M. Krap	One more little question and I am done.
Mme. Krap	(Sitting down again) I am late.
M. Krap	Oh *them*, they can wait. (A silence) How many times did you want to get rid of it?
Mme. Krap	(Under her breath) Three times.
M. Krap	And that yielded nothing?
Mme. Krap	Only discomforts.
M. Krap	Only discomforts! (Pause) Then you said — let's see — what are those nice words you had?
Mme. Krap	Nice words?
M. Krap	Why of course — let's see — *since it is here* — ?
Mme. Krap	*Let's keep it, since it is here.*
M. Krap	(Animatedly) That is it! That is it! *Let's keep it since it is here!* (Pause) We were on the water. Your oarsman had a knife. I was no longer rowing. The waves rocked us. (Pause) He too was rocked by the waves. (Pause) You are sure that he is mine?

MME. KRAP	(Upon reflection) There is — er — a seventy per cent chance.
M. KRAP	My stock is rising.
MME. KRAP	That is all?
M. KRAP	Ah yes, that is all.
MME. KRAP	(Getting up) You are not angry with me any more, Henri?
M. KRAP	Angry? On the contrary. I am very pleased with you, Violette, very pleased. You have really been just fine, utterly straightforward.
MME. KRAP	Enjoy your evening. (Goes)
M. KRAP	Violette!
MME. KRAP	(Stopping) Yes?
M. KRAP	You have no desire to kiss me?
MME. KRAP	Oh not now, Henri. I am *so* late.
M. KRAP	That is true.
MME. KRAP	(Mischievously) And then, I am still, you know, a little bit afraid of your knife. (Exit) (A rather long silence)
M. KRAP	Amuse the rubbernecks! (A silence. A knock. A silence. Another knock. A silence. Enter Jacques)
JACQUES	Monsieur is served.
M. KRAP	What more do you want?
JACQUES	Monsieur is served.
M. KRAP	You can say it.
JACQUES	Monsieur prefers that I serve him

	here?
M. KRAP	Serve him what?
JACQUES	Why, Monsieur's dinner.
M. KRAP	Ah yes, dinner. (Reflects) I will not be having dinner.
JACQUES	(Pained) Monsieur is having nothing?
M. KRAP	Not tonight.
JACQUES	Monsieur is not feeling well?
M. KRAP	Same as usual. (A silence)
JACQUES	Monsieur has no desire to hear a little music?
M. KRAP	Music?
JACQUES	That often does Monsieur good. (A silence) The Kopek Quartet is on right now, Monsieur. We are getting it in the pantry. Very nice program, Monsieur.
M. KRAP	What?
JACQUES	Schubert, Monsieur. (A silence) I could plug it in in the drawing room, Monsieur, and leave the doors open. Monsieur does not like it when the volume is too high.
M. KRAP	Do as you like. (Exit Jacques. Music. It is the Andante from the Quartet in A flat. For a good minute, if possible. Increasing agitation of M. Krap. Then, with

	all his might) Jacques! Jacques! (He tries to get up. Music) Jacques! (Music. Jacques runs in) Stop! Stop! (Exit Jacques. Music. Music stops.) What an abomination! (Enter Jacques)
JACQUES	Monsieur does not like it? (Increasing agitation of Monsieur Krap) I am dreadfully sorry, Monsieur. (A silence) Monsieur does not wish for anything?
M. KRAP	Do not leave me.
JACQUES	Of course not, Monsieur.
M. KRAP	Talk to me a little.
JACQUES	Is there something that is of particular interest to Monsieur. (A silence) Monsieur has seen the papers.
M. KRAP	I saw them yesterday.
JACQUES	What does Monsieur think of the new administration?
M. KRAP	No, no, not that. (A silence)
JACQUES	Monsieur has good news concerning Monsieur his son? (A silence)
M. KRAP	The wedding is when?
JACQUES	Monsieur means Marie and me?
M. KRAP	Yes.
JACQUES	We expect in a month or two, Monsieur.

M. KRAP	You already make love?
JACQUES	We — er — I — er — not precisely love, Monsieur.
M. KRAP	I have not offended you?
JACQUES	Oh Monsieur!...
M. KRAP	You are a bit obsequious, Jacques.
JACQUES	I rather like grovelling, Monsieur.
M. KRAP	Then you are right. (Marie appears at the door)
MARIE	Madame is asking for Monsieur on the telephone.
M. KRAP	Move a little this way, Marie. (Marie moves forward) Closer. (Marie stands next to the floor lamp) Turn around. (Marie turns around) She is cute.
MARIE	What am I to reply to Madame, Monsieur.
M. KRAP	That I am coming.
MARIE	Very good, Monsieur. (Exit)
M. KRAP	You must never be bored.
JACQUES	From time to time, Monsieur.
M. KRAP	Take the call.
JACQUES	Very good, Monsieur. (Exit. M. Krap motionless. Enter Jacques) Madame asks after Monsieur and sends word that Doctor Piouk regrets that Monsieur did not accompany Madame. Doctor Piouk had many things to say to Monsieur.

M. KRAP	You hung up?
JACQUES	Yes. I thought I was doing the right thing. (A silence)
M. KRAP	Jacques.
JACQUES	Yes, Monsieur.
M. KRAP	I would like you to kiss me.
JACQUES	Why certainly, Monsieur. On Monsieur's cheek?
M. KRAP	Where you like. (Jacques kisses Monsieur Krap)
JACQUES	Again, Monsieur?
M. KRAP	Thank you, no.
JACQUES	Very good, Monsieur. (He draws himself up again)
M. KRAP	Look. (Gives him a one-hundred-franc bill)
JACQUES	(Taking it) Oh, there was no need for that, Monsieur.
M. KRAP	You prickle.
JACQUES	Monsieur also prickles a little.
M. KRAP	You kiss well.
JACQUES	I do my best, Monsieur. (A silence)
M. KRAP	I should have been homosexual. (A silence) What do you think of it?
JACQUES	Of what, Monsieur?
M. KRAP	Of homosexuality.
JACQUES	I think that it must amount to

	nearly the same thing, Monsieur.
M. KRAP	You are cynical. (A silence)
JACQUES	Am I to remain close by Monsieur?
M. KRAP	No, you can abandon me.
JACQUES	Would Monsieur not be better off going to bed? (A silence) There is nothing else that I can do for Monsieur?
M. KRAP	No. Yes. Put out that abominable light.
JACQUES	Very good, Monsieur. (He switches off the floor lamp) I am leaving the small lamp on, Monsieur. (A silence) Good night, Monsieur.
M. KRAP	Good night. (Jacques goes) Leave the doors open.
JACQUES	Very good, Monsieur.
M. KRAP	So that you hear my cries.
JACQUES	Very good, M — Excuse me, Monsieur?
M. KRAP	Leave it open.
JACQUES	Very good, Monsieur. (He exits, uneasy) (M. Krap motionless)
M. KRAP	Curtain. (M. Krap motionless)

CURTAIN

ACT II

The next day. Late afternoon.

Victor's lodgings, a wretched furnished room whose sole piece of furniture is a folding bedstead.

Victor alone. Sordidly dressed, in his stocking feet, he moves back and forth. He stops near the footlights, looks at the audience, wants to speak, changes his mind, resume his walk. He again comes to a dead halt before the footlights, searches for the right words, ill at ease.

VICTOR	I must say ... I am not ... (He falls silent, resumes his walk, picks up a shoe and throws it through the windowpane. Enter immediately a Glazier, with all his gear and Victor's shoe in his hand. He tosses the shoe aside and sets to work) Impossible to break anything.
GLAZIER	But you broke it.
VICTOR	Neither can anything be lost. (Enter a young boy, with a box in his hand)
GLAZIER	That is my assistant. He is the one who carries the putty. Isn't that so, Michel?
MICHEL	Yes, papa.
GLAZIER	Yes, Monsieur.
MICHEL	Yes, Monsieur.
GLAZIER	You have the diamond?

MICHEL	No, Monsieur.
GLAZIER	Tsk! tsk! Quick! go find the diamond.
MICHEL	Yes, Monsieur. (Goes)
GLAZIER	Do not take away the putty! (Michel sets the box down near the window and exits) He was making off with the putty! (Scrapes) Little scatterbrain! (Scrapes) And the diamond. (Scrapes) What do you expect me to do without a diamond? (Turning toward Victor) Without a diamond I am nothing, Monsieur. (Enter Michel) How long does it take you. You have it?
MICHEL	Yes, Monsieur.
GLAZIER	Come around that way. Right near me. Make ready.
MICHEL	Yes, monsieur.
GLAZIER	I do not speak like a glazier, eh?
VICTOR	I do not know.
GLAZIER	You can trust me.
VICTOR	They sent you to spy on me?
GLAZIER	You wouldn't have broken the window then I wouldn't be here. (A silence. The Glazier is working) Do you not see, Monsieur, what must be admired about me is that I am useless.
VICTOR	You are of use in repairing my windowpane.

GLAZIER	All right, but you will break it again tomorrow. That is, I hope so.
VICTOR	As for me I break it in vain and as for you you repair it in vain.
GLAZIER	That is it!
VICTOR	It would be simplest not to begin.
GLAZIER	(Turning around) Ah Monsieur, now don't start talking nonsense. (Enter Madame Karl, an old woman)
MME. KARL	You broke the pane.
GLAZIER	His shoe, Madame, went clean through.
MME. KARL	The general's wife.
VICTOR	The general's wife?
MME. KARL	Yes.
VICTOR	Tell her that I went out.
MME. KARL	I told her. She does not want to leave.
VICTOR	Then let her stay.
MME. KARL	She is on her way up.
VICTOR	But she must be stopped!
MME. KARL	She has two blokes with her. Her chauffeur and another one.
VICTOR	I am going down.
MME. KARL	It is too late. (She goes out on the landing, comes back) She is on the fourth floor. She's puffing.
VICTOR	She's alone?
MME. KARL	I am telling you there are two

	blokes with her.
GLAZIER	Her chauffeur and another one, unidentified.
VICTOR	What's to be done?
GLAZIER	Hide.
VICTOR	Where?
GLAZIER	Under the bed.
VICTOR	You think so?
GLAZIER	Hurry! hurry! under the bed. (Victor hides under the bed)
MME. KARL	There she is. (Enter Mme. Meck. She searches Victor out with her eyes) I told you that he was not in.
GLAZIER	Allow me, Madame, to identify myself. I am supposed to be the glazier. And here we have young Michel, my supposed assistant. He is the one who carries the putty. Say hello to the lady, Michel. (Exit Madame Karl)
MICHEL	Hello, Madame.
MME. MECK	You have not seen Monsieur Krap?
GLAZIER	Monsieur Krap?
MME. MECK	The young man who lives here.
GLAZIER	Ah, the young man who lives here.
MME. MECK	You have not seen him?
GLAZIER	Yes, Madame.
MME. MECK	Where is he?
GLAZIER	He is under the bed, Madame, as

	in Molière's day. (Victor comes out from under the bed) You should have stayed there.
MME. MECK	Where is the method to this madness?
GLAZIER	It is with a view to public enter-tainment and refreshment, Ma-dame.
VICTOR	What do you want of me?
MME. MECK	He is cute, this little fellow. Come and say hello to me, my little gentleman. You would think he was a real little man.
GLAZIER	I would ask that you leave my assistant alone, Madame. He has already said hello. Don't you see that he is holding the putty?
MME. MECK	You are hardly very pleasant.
GLAZIER	There is a time for work, Madame, and there is a time for pleasant-ries. Michel must learn to tell the difference between them, early on.
MME. MECK	It is your son?
GLAZIER	When I am working I have no family, Madame.
MME. MECK	You call that working? You just chatter.
GLAZIER	My brain works non-stop.
MME. MECK	(To Victor) He resembles your poor papa a little when he was

	younger.
GLAZIER	Is that true?
MME. MECK	Don't you be concerning yourself with us.
GLAZIER	But you are concerning yourselves with me.
MME. MECK	(To Victor) You are not offering to get me a chair?
VICTOR	There is no chair.
MME. MECK	Last time there was one.
VICTOR	There are none left. (Mme. Meck sits down on the bed) What do you want?
MME. MECK	The resemblance is striking, really.
VICTOR	You are bringing me money?
MME. MECK	I have come to see you.
VICTOR	I am going out.
MME. MECK	I will go with you. (She gets up) (Victor goes to the door, opens it, is left momentarily speechless, goes out on the landing)
VICTOR'S VOICE	Madame Karl! (A silence) Madame Karl! (Victor comes back in and closes the door)
MME. MECK	So you are not going out?
VICTOR	Not right away. (Mme Meck sits down again) Who is that man on the landing?
MME. MECK	It is Joseph.
VICTOR	He is with you?

MME. MECK	He is a fifth-rate wrestler. Ludovic employed him from time to time.
VICTOR	He is with you?
MME. MECK	Yes, Victor, he is with me. (The Glazier goes to the door, opens it, looks out)
GLAZIER	Come look, Michel. (Michel goes to the door. Both of them look out for quite some time. The Glazier gently closes the door once more and goes back to his work. Victor follows him) That thing's foot must be a good size fifteen.
MICHEL	What does he have on his nose, papa?
GLAZIER	Monsieur.
MICHEL	Monsieur.
GLAZIER	I do not know, Michel, what he has on his nose. There are so many things that you can have on your nose. Ask him, if you want to know. Or rather ask this nice lady, that would be more advisable.
MICHEL	What does he have on his nose, Madame?
MME. MECK	It is the result of a bite, child.
MICHEL	It is a dog that bit him, Madame?
MME. MECK	No, child, it is a man like him, a fellow creature.
MICHEL	Why that he bit him, Madame?

MME. MECK	To force him to loosen his hold, child.
GLAZIER	Enough! enough! This is getting us nowhere. Hand me the tape measure.
MICHEL	But you are the one who has it, Monsieur.
GLAZIER	That is true. (He begins to take a measurement)
VICTOR	Why is that man with you?
MME. MECK	To carry you off by force, should the need arise.
VICTOR	By force?
MME. MECK	You are hardly to be moved by reason, I believe. (Enter Mme. Karl)
MME. KARL	What do you want?
VICTOR	I would like my bill. I am leaving.
MME. KARL	What did you say?
VICTOR	I said I am leaving and that I would like my bill.
MME. KARL	You must give a week's notice.
VICTOR	You make up a bill that seems fair to you. I am leaving here today.
MME. KARL	What is your complaint?
VICTOR	I am more than willing to respond, Madame Karl. My complaint is that I am being disturbed without stop. Yesterday it was my mother, today it is the general's wife, tomorrow it will be my

	fiancée. I cannot even break my windowpane without a glazier's turning up and setting about repairing it, with despairing slowness.
MME. KARL	You should not have given out the address.
VICTOR	I did not give it out. They found it.
MME. KARL	But everywhere you go they will find you the same old story.
GLAZIER	That is not a sure thing.
MME. KARL	(To Mme. Meck) You cannot leave him alone?
MME. MECK	Mind your own business.
VICTOR	Madame Karl, be nice, bring me the bill. It is pointless to argue with these people.
MME. KARL	It is a disgrace. (She goes)
VICTOR	Oh, Madame Karl.
MME. KARL	What?
VICTOR	Is Thérèse downstairs?
MME. KARL	Yes.
VICTOR	Ask her to go get an officer and bring him back here.
MME. KARL	An officer? What for? I do not want cops in my house.
VICTOR	This lady is trespassing in my place of residence.
MME. KARL	You are big enough to throw her out.

VICTOR	She got a bodyguard to come along with her. He is on the landing and only waiting for the signal to step in.
MME. MECK	Joseph! (Enter Joseph) Do what you have to do!
JOSEPH	It is him?
MME. MECK	Yes.
JOSEPH	(Taking Victor by the arm) Come along.
VICTOR	Help!
MME. KARL	Help!
JOSEPH	Shut your trap! (He pushes her)
VICTOR	Let me go! (He struggles feebly. Joseph drags him toward the door)
GLAZIER	(To Michel) Hand me the hammer.
MICHEL	But you are the one who has it, Monsieur.
GLAZIER	That is true. (He gets closer to Joseph and strikes him on the skull with the hammer. Joseph falls)
MME. MECK	This is ridiculous. (The Glazier goes back to his work)
MME. KARL	(Going) I am going to get an officer.
MME. MECK	He has killed him.
VICTOR	There is no longer any need, Madame Karl.

MME. KARL	We must lodge a complaint.
VICTOR	Tell the chauffeur to come up.
MME. KARL	He struck me.
VICTOR	The chauffeur, Madame Karl, the chauffeur. You will be compensated.
MME. KARL	This is no way to behave. (Exit)
MME. MECK	The violence has miscarried.
VICTOR	You make my life impossible. You heap shame and ridicule upon me. Go away.
MME. MECK	Life? What life? You are dead.
VICTOR	The dead are not hunted down.
MME. MECK	You know that your aunt is in Paris?
VICTOR	My mother told me.
MME. MECK	She has married a —
VICTOR	My mother told me.
MME. MECK	You know that your mother's heart is broken because of you.
VICTOR	Yes, she told me. Go away.
MME. MECK	And you do not mind.
VICTOR	I cannot help it.
MME. MECK	You can go back home.
VICTOR	I cannot go back home.
MME. MECK	You can live differently.
VICTOR	I cannot live differently.
MME. MECK	You know that Olga is sick with grief.
VICTOR	Yes, she told me and my mother

	has confirmed it.
MME. MECK	You no longer have any feeling for her.
VICTOR	No.
MME. MECK	Or for anybody.
VICTOR	No.
MME. MECK	Except for yourself.
VICTOR	Neither.
GLAZIER	It is taking shape.
MME. MECK	With what are you going to pay that bill?
VICTOR	With the money I have left.
MME. MECK	And then?
VICTOR	I will manage.
MME. MECK	Your father is dead. (A silence)
GLAZIER	Answer, will you please! (A knock. Enter Thomas)
VICTOR	Take care of your colleague. (He goes to the window)
THOMAS	Madame?
MME. MECK	See if he is breathing. Used as you are to engines.
THOMAS	(Having examined Joseph) Yes, Madame.
MME. MECK	He is breathing?
THOMAS	Yes, Madame.
MME. MECK	Pull him out on the landing.
THOMAS	Very good, Madame. (He pulls Joseph out on the landing, comes

	back)
MME. MECK	Try to revive him.
THOMAS	Very good, Madame.
MME. MECK	As soon as he can walk both of you go down and wait for me in the car.
THOMAS	Very good, Madame. (Exit) (A silence)
MME. MECK	Victor! (A silence) You heard me? Your father is dead.
VICTOR	(Turning around) Yes. When did he die?
MME. MECK	You are not going to tell me that that is of interest to you.
VICTOR	The time is of interest to me.
MME. MECK	He died last night, in his arm-chair.
VICTOR	But at what time?
MME. MECK	He was alive at eight o'clock. Jacques claims it to be so. And he was found dead toward midnight.
VICTOR	Who found him?
MME. MECK	Your poor mother.
VICTOR	At midnight?
MME. MECK	Approximately.
VICTOR	He was stiff?
MME. MECK	You are completely unnatural. (A silence) Your mother is prostrate.
GLAZIER	(To Michel) The diamond. (To Victor) There is no table?

VICTOR	No.
GLAZIER	So much the worse. (He starts to cut his glass on the floor)
VICTOR	(To Mme. Meck) Go away. (A knock. Enter Thomas)
THOMAS	I cannot revive him, Madame.
MME. MECK	He is still breathing?
THOMAS	Yes, Madame, but I cannot revive him.
MME. MECK	He is doubtless too heavy for you to be able to carry him.
THOMAS	I am afraid so, Madame.
MME. MECK	(To Victor) Wouldn't you like to help Thomas carry Joseph to the car?
VICTOR	No.
MME. MECK	(To the Glazier) And you? (A silence) Glazier!
GLAZIER	(Without turning around, while working) Madame?
MME. MECK	Wouldn't you like to help Thomas carry Joseph to the car?
GLAZIER	No, Madame, I would not.
MME. MECK	Well, then, Thomas, we must call an ambulance.
THOMAS	Very good, Madame. (Exit)
VICTOR	(To Mme. Meck) Go away.
MME. MECK	But now you can throw me out.
VICTOR	I am loath to touch you.
MME. MECK	(Getting down on her knees)

	Victor! Come back home! With me! In the Delage!
VICTOR	Get up.
MME. MECK	Help me. (Victor helps her get up, with his finger tips) The will —
GLAZIER	Shit! I cut it too small.
VICTOR	(To the Glazier) Just leave it.
GLAZIER	(Grandiloquently) I will repair that windowpane even if I have to spend the rest of my life at it.
MME. MECK	It is to be unsealed tomorrow, after the funeral.
GLAZIER	Hand me the tape measure.
MICHEL	But you are the one who has it.
GLAZIER	Monsieur.
MICHEL	Monsieur.
GLAZIER	That is true.
MME. MECK	Your mother is prostrate. (A silence) She cries out for you. (A silence) Her only support! (Glazier's hilarity, causing him to drop his tape measure)
GLAZIER	Hand me the tape measure. (Michel hands it to him)
VICTOR	(To Mme. Meck) Go away. (He picks up her bag and holds it out to her, picks up her umbrella and uses it to push her toward the door)
MME. MECK	Wretch!

Victor	(Still pushing) Go.
Mme. Meck	Give me my umbrella.
Victor	Go on, out. (He pushes her out, gives her the umbrella, closes the door, goes and sits back down on the bed)
	(A silence)
Glazier	She will come back.
Victor	(Half-turning toward the audience, with a helpless gesture) I —
Glazier	Now for a little peace and quiet.
Victor	Are you going to be much longer?
Glazier	The thing is I am not seeing straight any more.
Victor	Go away.
Glazier	I am going to turn the light on. (He goes to the switch and turns it on and off without success) It just needs the bulb. Michel, quick go get a bulb.
Michel	Yes, Monsieur. (Exit)
Glazier	(Approaching the bed) You do not have much of a tolerance for things made of glass.
Victor	Go away.
Glazier	Oh I'm the type, you know, the minute I put my nose to the grindstone, nothing stops me any more. What can you do, that's me.
Victor	If I had the courage I would try to

	throw you out.
GLAZIER	But you are afraid?
VICTOR	Yes.
GLAZIER	Of what?
VICTOR	Of pain. (A silence)
GLAZIER	You know, it is time that you explained yourself.
VICTOR	Explain myself?
GLAZIER	Well, yes. It cannot go on like this.
VICTOR	But I am at a loss to understand. Besides, I have nothing to say to you. Who are you? I do not know you. Get lost. (Pause) And out.
GLAZIER	Now, now, it would do you good to explain yourself a bit.
VICTOR	(With a howl) I tell you I am at a loss to understand!
GLAZIER	Explain yourself, no, I am not saying that, I did not put it right. Define yourself, there. It is time that you defined yourself a little. You are around like a sort of — what is the way to say it? — like a sort of ooze. Like a sanies, there. Take on a little contour, for the love of God.
VICTOR	Why.
GLAZIER	So that all this may look like it holds water. You have been impossible up until now. Nobody will be

	able to believe in it. Why, my friend, you are quite simply nothing, poor fellow.
VICTOR	It is perhaps time that somebody was quite simply nothing.
GLAZIER	But of course, but of course, I know, I have heard that routine. All that is nothing but words. Listen. When she — (Enter Michel) — when she told — you, what is it you want?
MICHEL	The bulb, Monsieur.
GLAZIER	So, put it in! When she told you —
MICHEL	Where is it have to be put in, Monsieur?
GLAZIER	Where is it have to be put in! Why in the — in the — in the whatsit, what else, not in your behind, in the — in the SOCKET, there we go, put it in the socket, and timeclock it, don't half-cock it. (Pause) Deep down only words interest me. I am a poet who would rather not know it. (To Michel) So, you are getting there?
MICHEL	I am not getting there, Monsieur.
GLAZIER	You can call me papa right now, it is break time.
MICHEL	It is too high, papa.
GLAZIER	Get up on a chair.
MICHEL	There is no chair, papa.

GLAZIER	That is true. Then get up on a box. (Michel drags the toolbox under the socket, gets up onto it, puts in the bulb, gets down) Now turn on the light. (Michel goes to the door, turns on the switch, the bulb lights up) It is working.
VICTOR	(Half-rising) I am going.
GLAZIER	Turn it off. (Michel turns it off. Victor drops back on the bed) Come here. Bring the box. (The Glazier sits down on the box opposite Victor, puts his arm around Michel and props him up against him)
MICHEL	What is the matter with him, the Monsieur, papa?
GLAZIER	Who is telling you there is something the matter with him?
MICHEL	He looks funny.
GLAZIER	He is funny.
MICHEL	It is because his papa died?
GLAZIER	How do you know that his papa died?
MICHEL	It is the fat lady who said so.
GLAZIER	Maybe she lied. (Pause) Take a good look at him, Michel.
MICHEL	Why is that, the lady, she would have lied, papa?
GLAZIER	So he would go back with her, don't you know. Then home at

last they would have locked him up. (Pause) Take a good look at him. (Pause) You will not be like that when you grow up, how about it, Michel?

MICHEL   Oh no, papa.
(Enter Madame Karl)

MME. KARL   (To the Glazier) You there, you still haven't finished?

GLAZIER   No, Madame, I still haven't finished, and I am nowhere near finishing either, at the rate it is going.

MME. KARL   (To Victor) Here is the bill. (Moves up to the bed) Here. (Victor sluggishly takes the bill and holds it in his hand without looking at it.) So you are leaving, yes or no? (A silence) You are ill?

GLAZIER   Let him think it over.

VICTOR   (Straining) Madame Karl, I ask only to remain here, but I must be left alone.

GLAZIER   They are holding open house here. It is not to be believed. Nobody even knocks.

MME. KARL   What can I do about it when they turn up with thugs. They all know he is here. He should just have not given out the address.

GLAZIER   Speaking of Tarzan, he is still on the landing?

MME. KARL	No, he left.
GLAZIER	In the ambulance?
MME. KARL	No, he left all by himself on foot.
GLAZIER	(Rubbing his hands) Now for a little peace and quiet!
VICTOR	You would not have another room?
MME. KARL	What difference would that make?
VICTOR	You would be saying that I am no longer in your place and then I would be in the other room.
MME. KARL	All the rooms are taken.
GLAZIER	And why don't you lock yourself in?
VICTOR	There is no lock.
GLAZIER	No lock! (To Mme. Karl) You are not ashamed, to rent out rooms without locks?
MME. KARL	He should not have taken it. No one forced him to.
GLAZIER	But you mean you don't see which — what a wreck you are dealing with? (To Michel) Quick go get a lock.
MICHEL	Yes, papa.
GLAZIER	Monsieur.
MICHEL	Yes, Monsieur. (Exit)
GLAZIER	We are going to take care of it for you.
VICTOR	They'll break down the door.
MME. KARL	So? You are leaving yes or no?

GLAZIER	But give him room to breathe, for Pete's sake!
VICTOR	I will tell you that in a little while.
MME. KARL	I am giving you an hour. Then I hang up the vacancy sign. (Exit) (A silence)
GLAZIER	You hadn't thought of that.
VICTOR	Leave me alone. Do not say another word. Do what you have to do and go away.
GLAZIER	Yes, but first, tell me, you hadn't thought of that?
VICTOR	Of course I had.
GLAZIER	Of having a lock installed?
VICTOR	But of course.
GLAZIER	But I am not talking about that! I mean you hadn't thought that the old girl could be lying when she told you your father was dead.
VICTOR	She did not lie. (A silence. Enter Michel)
GLAZIER	Where were you dawdling this time?
MICHEL	I did not dawdle, papa.
GLAZIER	You have the lock?
MICHEL	Yes, Monsieur.
GLAZIER	And two keys.
MICHEL	Yes, Monsieur.
GLAZIER	Good. (He gets up. To Victor) As for you, I have nothing more to say to you. I have seen amateurs,

but never anybody as bad as you.
If you'd had your heart set on
being hooted down, you could
not have done better. The answers
are put in your mouth and you
come out with the exact opposite.
Have you any more feeling for
your mother? No. Or for your
fiancée? No. Or for anybody? No.
Only for yourself? None either.
But what's with this bull? Feeling
is what is needed, God damn it!
Why, naturally you love your
mother, why naturally you love
your fiancée, *but* — BUT — you
have duties, with regard to yourself, your work, science, the party,
and who knows what else, which
make of you a man apart, the
being as exception, which forbid
you the tender bonds of the
family, of passion, fits you out in a
mask made of cellophane. Feeling! feeling, then going above and
beyond, there you have what's
needed. To sacrifice everything, to
the idée fixe, to the priesthood!
At that point you begin to live.
Nobody is any longer of a mind to
lynch you. You are the poor young
man, the heroic young man. You
are seen croaking like a dog at
thirty, at thirty-three, drained by

your labors, by your discoveries, eaten away by radium, laid low by the sleepless nights, by the privations, died on mission, shot by Franco, shot by Stalin. Your praises are sung. Mother is dying of grief, girl friend as well, it doesn't matter, men like you are needed, men with an ideal, above comforts, above pity, so that toffee may go on being sold. (Imitating him) No — no — she told me — I want nothing — I can do nothing — I feel nothing — I am nothing — leave me alone — go away — please — I implore you. Shit! (To Michel) The light. But what is your merit?

VICTOR What?
(Michel turns on the light)

GLAZIER I am asking you what merit you have rotting in this hole?

VICTOR I do not know.

GLAZIER I do not know, I do not know. Ah! go hide in a corner.

VICTOR I would like to.

GLAZIER (To Michel) Give me the tape measure.

MICHEL But you are the one who has it, Monsieur.

GLAZIER (Thunderingly) No, I am not the one who has it! (To Victor) Where

	do you draw the courage and strength to evict old ladies, with the pokes of an umbrella?
VICTOR	I look out for my welfare, when I can.
GLAZIER	Your welfare! What welfare?
VICTOR	My freedom.
GLAZIER	Your freedom! It is beautiful, your freedom. Freedom to do what?
VICTOR	To do nothing.
GLAZIER	(Controlling himself with difficulty, to Michel) The tape measure.
MICHEL	Here it is, Monsieur.
GLAZIER	What do we do? Do we finish the windowpane or do we do the lock or do we drop everything?
MICHEL	I am hungry, papa.
GLAZIER	You are hungry, papa. Then let's do the lock first. (He sets to work. A silence. He sings)

> *Beautiful is France,*
> *Her destinies are blessed,*

(To Michel) Sing!

| GLAZIER ⎫ MICHEL ⎭ | (Together) |

> *Beautiful is France,*
> *Her destinies are blessed,*
> *As one we advance,*

As hers we live best.

Over the mountains, o —

(Enter Mademoiselle Skunk. She goes and stands in front of Victor, still seated on the bed)

MLLE. SKUNK	Hello, Victor.
VICTOR	Hello.
MLLE. SKUNK	Who is that man?
VICTOR	He is a glazier.
MLLE. SKUNK	What is he doing here?
VICTOR	He is repairing the windowpane.
MLLE. SKUNK	You broke the windowpane?
VICTOR	What?
MLLE. SKUNK	You are the one who broke the windowpane?
VICTOR	Yes.
MLLE. SKUNK	How? Why?
VICTOR	I do not know.
GLAZIER	With one of his brogues, Mademoiselle, and with malice aforethought. All hopes are allowed.
MLLE. SKUNK	Why did you do that?
VICTOR	What?
MLLE. SKUNK	Why did you break the windowpane?
VICTOR	I do not know.
GLAZIER	Come, Michel. (Exit the Glazier and Michel)
MLLE. SKUNK	You do not want to kiss me?
VICTOR	No.

MLLE. SKUNK	I am not good-looking?
VICTOR	I do not know.
MLLE. SKUNK	At one time you found me good-looking. You wanted to sleep with me.
VICTOR	At one time.
MLLE. SKUNK	You do not want to sleep with me any more?
VICTOR	No.
MLLE. SKUNK	With whom then?
VICTOR	What?
MLLE. SKUNK	Whom do you want to sleep with now.
VICTOR	With nobody.
MLLE. SKUNK	But it is not possible? (A silence) You are not being honest! (A silence) You know that I love you?
VICTOR	You have told me.
MLLE. SKUNK	You have no pity for me?
VICTOR	No.
MLLE. SKUNK	You want me to go away.
VICTOR	Yes.
MLLE. SKUNK	And that I never come back any more?
VICTOR	Yes. (A silence.)
MLLE. SKUNK	What has changed you so?
VICTOR	I do not know.
MLLE. SKUNK	You were not like this before. What has made you like this?

VICTOR	I do not know. (Pause) I have always been like this.
MLLE. SKUNK	Oh no! It isn't true. You loved me. You worked. You joked around with your father. You travelled. You —
VICTOR	That was bluffing. Besides, enough. Go away. (Enter the Glazier and Michel)
GLAZIER	I wanted to be discreet, tactful, a man of the world, but I see that it cannot be done. Hence I am taking up my work again. For every moment is precious. With your permission. (To Michel) Hand me the — (He finds it) Hold the door. (He starts working)
MLLE. SKUNK	Your father is dead.
VICTOR	Jeanne told me.
MLLE. SKUNK	Jeanne was here?
VICTOR	Yes.
MLLE. SKUNK	When?
VICTOR	A little while ago. (A silence)
MLLE. SKUNK	It makes no difference to you.
VICTOR	What?
MLLE. SKUNK	That your father is dead? (A silence) You know what he said to me last night? (A silence) He made me promise to look like I

was living so you too would look like you were living. I don't understand. (A silence) This is what I've come for, for you to explain to me what that means. (A silence) You understand what that means?

VICTOR   No.

MLLE. SKUNK   You don't even try.

VICTOR   No.

MLLE. SKUNK   Why.

VICTOR   Everything can be understood.

MLLE. SKUNK   Then explain to me.

VICTOR   (Furiously) No!
                (A silence)

MLLE. SKUNK   He asked me to kiss him. (Pause) I couldn't.

VICTOR   But you want me to be the one to kiss you.

GLAZIER   (Turning around) Well, well. There is perhaps something to be done thereabouts. It's not the line I would have taken, it will never amount to much, but it's perhaps better than nothing all the same. (To Mlle. Skunk) Don't you see, Mademoiselle, what he neither can nor wants to understand is that he is not credible. I cannot repeat it often enough. (Pause) But if it was out of love for his father that he — (He breaks off). No, that will get us nowhere.

Unless — (Pause) All right then, there's some feeling out to be done. If only to keep down the number of casualties. (To Mlle. Skunk) Scratch him a little there-abouts. Poor old guy, jeered at by his wife, abandoned by his son, his work a mockery, sick as a dog, and feeling the end is near, he asks you to kiss him and you don't want to. What next?

MLLE. SKUNK   I do not understand a word you are saying. You talk like him.

GLAZIER   Like who?

MLLE. SKUNK   Like his father.

GLAZIER   You don't say! At any rate. Handle it yourself. To work. Every moment is precious. (To Michel) Hold the door firm. Wedge it up good. With your foot. There. (He goes back to work)

MLLE. SKUNK   (To Victor) You understand what he means?

VICTOR   No. (A silence) Go away. I am tired.

MLLE. SKUNK   (Getting up) I am going. (A silence) You're staying here?

VICTOR   I am going to try to sleep.

MLLE. SKUNK   No, I mean in future, you are going to stay here?

VICTOR   No, I am going to go somewhere else.

MLLE. SKUNK	Where?
VICTOR	I do not know. (A silence)
MLLE. SKUNK	Marguerite has come back. (A silence) She has gotten married. (A silence) To a doctor. (Victor stretches out) He is making advances to me. (A silence) You know what he said to me? (A silence. Mlle. Skunk fidgets) Well answer, for once!
VICTOR	I do not understand.
MLLE. SKUNK	What? What is it you don't understand?
VICTOR	What you want to know.
MLLE. SKUNK	But I do not want to know anything. I only want you to listen to me.
VICTOR	I am listening. I thought you were leaving.
MLLE. SKUNK	I told him I should like to be dead. He told me that was easy and that he would be happy to help me with it.
GLAZIER	Funny advances.
VICTOR	Who?
MLLE. SKUNK	The doctor.
VICTOR	Which doctor?
MLLE. SKUNK	Why, Marguerite's husband. I just told you.
VICTOR	I didn't know that she was married.

(A silence)

GLAZIER   Watch out! Somebody's coming
up! (He goes out on the landing,
comes back) It is a society woman.
I saw her hat. I smelled her per-
fume. As she comes up the stairs,
she is being careful not to touch
the banister. She is not alone. (He
closes the door and leans against
it. A silence. A knock. A silence.
Another knock. A silence. A push.
The Glazier, setting his back
against the door, resists the push.
He motions to Michel to help
him. Michel helps him) She is as
strong as an ox. (Pause) To open,
or not to open, that is the — (To
Michel) — well?

MICHEL   That is the question.

GLAZIER   It is starting again. (To Michel)
Push. (They push)
(To Mlle. Skunk) Help us.

VOICE   Open up!

MLLE. SKUNK   It is him!

GLAZIER   Who?

MLLE. SKUNK   The doctor!
(The Glazier moves abruptly away
from the door which opens im-
petuously, knocking over Michel.
Dr. Piouk rushes into the room
and lands on his knees. Same
business for Mme. Piouk who

	follows him. Mme. Meck in the doorway. Dr. Piouk gets up)
DR. PIOUK	(To the Glazier) Is it you who are the perpetrator of that schoolboy prank?
GLAZIER	Have to keep the rubbernecks well entertained.
MME. PIOUK	Help me. (Mlle. Skunk helps her to get back up)
DR. PIOUK	You didn't hurt yourself, my darling?
GLAZIER	(To Michel) You didn't hurt yourself, my darling?
MICHEL	No, papa.
GLAZIER	Then, up with you, dumb-bell. (Michel gets back up)
DR. PIOUK	Who is this man?
MLLE. SKUNK	He is a workman.
DR. PIOUK	(To the Glazier) What business is this of yours?
GLAZIER	What business of mine. (Ponders) What business of mine, precisely. (Strokes his chin)
DR. PIOUK	Get out!
GLAZIER	(To Michel) The hammer.
MME. MECK	Do not provoke him. He is a violent man. (Michel hands over the hammer)
DR. PIOUK	I fear nobody.
MME. PIOUK	Where is Victor?
MLLE. SKUNK	He is around here somewhere.

GLAZIER	And the chisel.
MME. PIOUK	(Rushing over) Victor! (Michel hands over the chisel)
MME. MECK	(To Mlle. Skunk) What are you doing here?
MLLE. SKUNK	I wonder.
MME. PIOUK	Come and see, André. (Dr. Piouk gets closer to the bed)
DR. PIOUK	That is Victor, there? (A silence. Mme. Meck, Mlle. Skunk, Dr. and Mme. Piouk around the bed. Dr. Piouk takes out his watch, bends over, takes Victor's wrist. A silence. Victor jumps up, elbows his way through the group, looks for his shoes, finds one, sticks his foot in, looks for the other)
VICTOR	(Piteously) My shoe!
GLAZIER	(To Michel) Where did you put Monsieur's shoe?
MICHEL	But you are the one who had it, Monsieur.
GLAZIER	(Forcefully) Look for it! (Michel looks for the shoe, finds it, proffers it to Victor who snatches it from him and exits, one shoe on his foot, the other in his hand, returns immediately, runs to the footlights, wants to speak, cannot, gives way to a gesture of helplessness, exits gesturing madly. A silence) What vivacity! (A pause)

	He forgot the bill. (To Michel) Quick, take the bill and go after him.
MICHEL	The bill?
GLAZIER	(Angrily) How old are you?
MICHEL	Ten, papa.
GLAZIER	And you still do not know what a bill is?
MICHEL	(On the verge of tears) No, papa.
GLAZIER	The check! The invoice! The note! There! (He pushes him) Go! Step on it! (Michel picks up the bill and exits running) He is my son. He is still a halfwit.
DR. PIOUK	That does not surprises me.
GLAZIER	Ah, that does not surprise you. (He moves forward, hammer and chisel very much in evidence)
DR. PIOUK	(Drawing back) Back! I am armed!
MME. PIOUK	(Running toward her husband) André! Come! Let's get out of here!
GLAZIER	(Still moving forward) Step aside, Madame.
MME. MECK	It's getting stagey. Coming, Olga?
MME. PIOUK	Come, André, don't do anything rash!
GLAZIER	(Changing his mind) After all — who knows — it may serve — although I do not see how. (To Dr.

Piouk) Calm down, Doctor, calm down. Are we dumb beasts? Is it all about us? No. About what then? This is what we must try to figure out. Tell me — (The Glazier takes Dr. Piouk by the arm and draws him aside)

MME. MECK   Olga, Marguerite, come. (Enter Mme. Krap in deep mourning)

MME. PIOUK }
MME. MECK }   (Together) Violette!

MME. KRAP   My son! Where is he?

MLLE. SKUNK   Gone.

MME. KRAP   Gone!

MLLE. SKUNK   Gone.

MME. KRAP   (Dropping back on the bed) Where?

MLLE. SKUNK   We do not know. (Enter Michel, the bill in his hand)

MICHEL   Papa!

GLAZIER   (To Dr. Piouk) Don't you agree? (To Michel) You, what do you want?

MICHEL   I did not find him, papa.

GLAZIER   You did not find him?

MICHEL   No, papa. I ran all over, papa. It is not my fault, papa.

GLAZIER   Oh, enough with your papas!

MME. KRAP	Who is this man? (The Glazier goes and stands in front of her) Who are you? You are a friend of my son's? What are you doing here? What is making you look at me that way? (She puts her hands in front of her face. She moves her hands away) Who are you?
GLAZIER	I am the glazier, Madame. Allow me to offer my condolences.
MME. KRAP	Your condolences!
GLAZIER	Yes, Madame, my condolences. (An interval) Deeply felt.
MME. KRAP	Then you know! (An interval) Where have I seen you?
GLAZIER	I do not know, Madame. On the street, perhaps, by chance. Or you are confusing me, perhaps, with another person. (Mme. Meck leans over and whispers in Mme. Krap's ear)
MME. KRAP	You think so? (She looks at the Glazier) Perhaps — yes — you are right — my God! (She weeps)
MME. MECK	Violette!
MME. KRAP	(Drying her eyes, to the Glazier) You are a friend of my son's.
GLAZIER	Er — not yet, Madame.
MME. KRAP	You saw him today?
MME. PIOUK	But we all saw him, Violette.
MME. KRAP	You told me that —

MME. MECK	But of course, Violette.
MME. KRAP	What did he say? (A silence. Dr. Piouk is laughing to himself)
MME. PIOUK	André!
MME. KRAP	Where is he? (A silence. Mme. Krap goes into a panic) He is not dead? (A silence) He is dead! He is dead!
GLAZIER	He was not four, five minutes ago, not what the living call dead.
MME. KRAP	He is alive!
GLAZIER	His heart is beating, that's for sure.
MME. KRAP	How was he?
GLAZIER	On edge, Madame, on edge. He does not seem to be very fond of company, not even that of his kith and kin.
MME. KRAP	And he knew that —
MME. MECK	But of course, Violette, I told him, with every possible precaution you can imagine.
MME. KRAP	So? (A silence)
MME. MECK	He is ill, Violette, he must not be judged too harshly.
MME. KRAP	(Dolefully) Here I was thinking I would find him very much alone: I wanted to make one last attempt. You have botched every-

	thing!
MME. MECK	It was with good intentions, Violette.
MME. KRAP	(In the same way) After yesterday I thought there was nothing more to be done. Then the death (She sniffles) of Henri, don't you know, I thought that he would listen to me perhaps. (Pause) I am all alone right now (She sniffles), all alone (She weeps).
MLLE. SKUNK	Listen, Violette, you would be better off going home. You will need all your strength for tomorrow.
DR. PIOUK	Go back with her, Marguerite.
MME. MECK	Come, darling.
MME. KRAP	My son! I want my son!
MLLE. SKUNK	Leave it to us.
MME. KRAP	Bring him to me!
MME. MECK	Come! (She draws Mme. Krap along toward the door)
MME. PIOUK	Coming, André?
DR. PIOUK	I will be right along, my darling. (He kisses her) Go with your sister, she needs you.
MME. PIOUK	There's nothing here for you to do.
MME. KRAP	Bring him back to me! (Exit Mmes. Krap and Meck)
DR. PIOUK	Yes, my darling. I will explain.

Hurry up and go. (He pushes her gently toward the door) You will see, everything will work out. (He pushes her out gently) See you very soon, my darling. (He shuts the door)

GLAZIER
The time that is lost with walk-ons!

MICHEL
(Emerging from a dark corner where the audience is presumed to have forgotten him) Papa!

GLAZIER
Now what do you want?

MICHEL
I would like to go home, papa. I am hungry.

GLAZIER
Will you just listen to this little snotnose? (To Dr. Piouk) He ate ten potatoes at noon and now he is hungry.
(To Michel) You are not ashamed?

MICHEL
I do not feel well, papa.

DR. PIOUK
He undoubtedly has worms.

GLAZIER
You hear that? You have worms. Come here. (Michel goes) Show the doctor your tongue. (Pause) Stick out your tongue, runt!
(Michel sticks out his tongue which Dr. Piouk examines with the aid of a small electric lamp)

DR. PIOUK
(Switching off the lamp) The mirror of the stomach.

GLAZIER
Well?

DR. PIOUK	It is yellow, coated and dry.
GLAZIER	(Giving Michel money) Go buy yourself a sandwich. And come back at once. You understand?
MICHEL	Yes, papa. (He goes)
GLAZIER	Buy two.
MICHEL	Yes, papa. (Exit)
GLAZIER	Ah, children.
DR. PIOUK	Now let us settle this question. We, Mademoiselle Skunk and I, have more to get done.
GLAZIER	Your wish is my command. What is it a question of exactly, in your opinion?
DR. PIOUK	It is a question, if I have indeed understood the different accounts that have been given me, by my wife, by my sister-in-law and by you, dear Mademoiselle, of a psychological state difficult to define.
GLAZIER	It's a good start.
DR. PIOUK	If you please. This young man, for reasons still to be determined, seems to have lost his taste for life. He was working — (To Mademoiselle Skunk) — he was writing, I believe?
MLLE. SKUNK	Yes. The critics said he would be talked about.
GLAZIER	That must have dealt him a low

	blow.
DR. PIOUK	Good. He was writing. He no longer writes. He was associating normally with his family. He has left and no longer wants to see them. He got engaged, which is normal at his age, to a ravishing girl, oh yes, oh yes, Mademoiselle, ravishing, and he denies her right of entry. (To the Glazier) Excuse me?
GLAZIER	Nothing.
DR. PIOUK	He was taking an interest in the inexhaustible variety of the Parisian scene, in art, in theater, in science, in politics, in every new school of philosophy, in the —
GLAZIER	Get to the point, get to the point.
DR. PIOUK	And he had made himself a veritable specialty out of the idle kings. Isn't that so, Mademoiselle? Good. All that is now dead for him, just as if it had never existed? Do I exaggerate, dear Mademoiselle?
MLLE. SKUNK	No.
DR. PIOUK	He travelled, for his amusement and for his edification. Now —
GLAZIER	Which class?
DR. PIOUK	Now he no longer leaves, for months on end, this (circling look) — this foul sty. He had

money, now —

GLAZIER All right, all right, we have understood.

DR. PIOUK If you interrupt me every minute, I have no choice but to leave. In fact, I ask nothing more.

GLAZIER But you go on and on. We are not asking you for a catalogue. He no longer does anything, he is no longer interested in anything, he no longer wants to see anybody, that's settled. Now what? What must be done to get him put up with?

DR. PIOUK Get him put up with?

GLAZIER But of course. It makes no sense, a creature like that. It does not hold water.

DR. PIOUK But get him put up with? By whom? No, it is quite simply a matter of coming to his assistance and, in coming to his assistance, of coming to the assistance of those closest to him and —

GLAZIER Oh no, oh no, you don't get it. Nobody gives a damn if he drops dead, provided that —

DR. PIOUK Monsieur, if you have something to say, something reasonable, which I strongly doubt, you will say it in a little while, when I myself have finished. You ask me my opinion, I am giving it to you. There is no arguing on that score. I never argue. Sorry. Am I to go on? Or am I to leave?

MLLE. SKUNK   Go on, go on, you are the only one saying things I can understand.

DR. PIOUK   Ah, Mademoiselle, if you only knew, if you only knew! (He woolgathers)

GLAZIER   Go ahead, go ahead, she will never know.

DR. PIOUK   Where was I?

GLAZIER   Raving right along, about the need to help him and, while helping him, to help his family and, while helping his family, to help who knows who else, quite the whole of mankind, probably. You must love mankind, Doctor.

DR. PIOUK   You are crude. No matter. Good. Yes. I was in effect saying that in helping him I would be helping those close to him and, first of all, you, dear Mademoiselle, so incomprehensibly forsaken, so cowardly, insanely abandoned. The problem thus reduces to this: finding a suitable means to — how should I put it? — to restore him to himself and therefore to others. (A silence) As for the means, I have it — (He pats his belly) — here.

MLLE. SKUNK   Oh Doctor, if only you could!

DR. PIOUK   Yes. (He reflects) When I was the director — There wouldn't be a chair over that way?

GLAZIER   No. He is no longer interested in chairs. But there is a bed, of all the objects that poison existence the only one he still tolerates. Ah, beds! Sit down.

DR. PIOUK   (With a glance toward the bed) Thank you. So much the worse. What was I saying?

MLLE. SKUNK   When you were the director —

DR. PIOUK   Oh yes. When I was the director of the Hospice Saint-Guy, in the Haute-Marne, every day, every other day rather, I would see an unbalanced person whose nationality was Romanian and who believed he was afflicted with — (He glances toward Mlle. Skunk, lowers his voice) — with syphilis. Need I say he was not.

GLAZIER   Of course you need to say it.

DR. PIOUK   He would ask me every time, in a desperate tone of voice, if I was bringing him the poison. The poison? I would say, which poison, my friend, and to do what with? To put an end to my torment, he

would reply. But my dear fellow, if you absolutely insist on putting an end to your torment, you have at your disposal all that is needed for that. Three times a day you eat in the refectory, surrounded by plates, cups, forks and even knives, with which to put an end to a thousand torments. Then he would get angry, saying that it behooved me, as his physician, and not him, to put an end to his torment. But what torment after all, I would say. There is nothing wrong with you. Fourteen physicians have examined you under conditions of the most thoroughgoing independence of each other and found nothing. Yes they have, yes they have, he would reply. I have — ahem — (Same business as before) syphilis and it is your duty to do away with me. It is on that note that our dialogue, always identical, would come to a close. (Pause) Up until the day I brought him the poison he had been clamoring for.
(A silence)

MLLE. SKUNK   (Gasping for breath) And then what?

DR. PIOUK   His recovery was swift.
(A silence)

GLAZIER	He wasn't a true madman.
DR. PIOUK	I will not waste my time arguing about that. (Pause) And Victor, he is a true madman? (A silence. All of a sudden Dr. Piouk has slightly disjointed gestures, starts a dance step, makes odd movements with his arms, like signals, in other words, such as suit the actor's fancy, then comes to a stop. Mild embarrassment) Yesterday I set forth, before the late lamented Monsieur Krap, a remarkable man, I might add, in his own way, the manner in which I view the problem of human existence, for a problem it is, in my opinion, despite the efforts today being made to demonstrate the contrary. (Pause) I will even say that I see no other. Not being an ant, for example, or a whale. (Pause) You were there, Mademoiselle.
MLLE. SKUNK	Yes.
DR. PIOUK	You see, I am not making up anything. I therefore said, plagued with questions, for I don't like to put myself too much in the picture, I said that I was taking up again on my own behalf the solution already put forth by numerous thinkers to this problem of consciousness and which

consists quite simply of suppressing the latter. I said it was the modalities of that suppression, the technical aspect, that interested me very particularly, for I am a man of action, and I pointed out some of the means best suited, in my view, to bringing it about with the utmost promptness and the least inconvenience. Need I say I don't believe in them one bit, not for a minute? I mean that life has cured me of all hope of seeing it end, on a grand scale. At the very most it could be curbed. (Pause) But I am a methodical man, in my own way, courageous, in a sense, and I venture to say upright, and I remain at the disposal of those who, while being of my opinion concerning them, surpass me in sadness and resolve.

MLLE. SKUNK But you want to kill him!

GLAZIER You think he needs you to end it all, assuming he wants to end it all?

DR. PIOUK My dear fellow, it is amazing the help people need in ceasing to be. You have no idea. You almost have to hold their hand. (Pause) Take my Romanian, for example. Did he need me to put an end to his torment? Of course not. What is more, he is now a cattle-dealer in Iassy. He writes to me from time to time. A postcard. He calls me his savior. His savior! Ha!

GLAZIER   There is no similarity. He believed he was gravely ill.

DR. PIOUK   I am in ignorance as to what this young man is complaining of exactly. Of something more severe, I think, than any given illness and assuredly more vague as well. I was told that he enjoys robust health. Let us assume that he is complaining quite simply of existing, of the life syndrome. It's conceivable, isn't it? We are no longer in the nineteenth century. We know how to look things full in the face. Good. I am putting him in the way of existing no more, of passing over, with the greatest smoothness, from the state of consciousness to that of pure extension —

MLLE. SKUNK   No! no! I won't allow it!

DR. PIOUK   (Breaking out) — while I'm telling him I will stay at his side to see to it that the transition is carried through without let. So, my dear friends, either he discovers good reasons — for he's a thinker, that's obvious — to go back among his fellow creatures

for the same old shit, or — (Expressive gesture) But rest assured it's more than likely he is as scummy as the rest of us.
(A silence. The Glazier walks up and down. Olga crushed. Dr. Piouk beaming)

MLLE. SKUNK   It's abominable. You mustn't!

DR. PIOUK   Mademoiselle, if I've been a little bit off in my own world, if I have minced words insufficiently, lay it to the account of an old enthusiasm, about to be snuffed out. For me to speak thus is to breathe another air, that of my youth, of my ardors, of my innocencies, before the black flag and the bowed skull. (Moved) Mademoiselle (He takes her chin and lifts it), look at me. Do I seem like an ogre? (He smiles hideously) Do be confident! I will save him! As I saved Verolesco.

MLLE. SKUNK   But if he takes it?

DR. PIOUK   What?

MLLE. SKUNK   The — the — poison.

DR. PIOUK   He will not take it.

MLLE. SKUNK   But if he wants to take it?

DR. PIOUK   Well — (Straining) — well, it is against my principles, but, to please you, well, we will prevent him. You see, dear Olga, yes, let me call you Olga, I am ready for anything to oblige you.

MLLE. SKUNK   But if we get there too late?

DR. PIOUK   (Laughing) It is easy to see this is not your department. How many things that pretty little head is unaware of! How many nasty things! The very idea! Why, I'll know immediately if he is serious or not. Even before I hand him the tablet.

MLLE. SKUNK   It's a tablet?
(Dr. Piouk takes a phial out of his vest pocket, rolls a tablet out into the palm of his hand, holds it out toward Mlle. Skunk who hesitates, then takes it)

DR. PIOUK   There.
(Enter Michel. He gives the Glazier a sandwich)

GLAZIER   You ate yours?

MICHEL   Yes, papa.

GLAZIER   You were gallivanting about.

MICHEL   No, papa.

GLAZIER   Hand over the change. (Michel gives him the change, which he counts) Good. Here, hold this. (He gives him back the sandwich) Take this too. (He gives him the hammer and chisel) Get over there and be quiet. (Michel goes and sits down on the toolbox,

	near the window)
MLLE. SKUNK	(Tearing herself away from gazing at the tablet) Quite so. (Dr. Piouk takes back the tablet, puts it back in the phial and puts the phial back in his pocket)
DR. PIOUK	Yes, quite so, that little thing, languor, rockabye, bottomless blanknesses, rock bottom, peace, standstill. What time is it. (He pulls out his watch) Five past five (He puts back his watch) My goodness!
MLLE. SKUNK	And what if you —
GLAZIER	(His mind made up) Agreed. It is not —
DR. PIOUK	(To the Glazier) Be quiet! (To Mlle. Skunk) You were saying?
MLLE. SKUNK	What if you gave him a simple aspirin?
DR. PIOUK	(Straightening up) Mademoiselle, I am only a poor Joe, but I do not trifle with sedatives. No. I don't get mixed up in things like that. Anything to please you, but not that. (A silence)
GLAZIER	I am set —
DR. PIOUK	Will this take long?
GLAZIER	Not as long as you.
DR. PIOUK	You've got five minutes.

GLAZIER	I am set within a viewpoint —
DR. PIOUK	One moment. May I? What is your stake in the matter? It is not very clear to me.
GLAZIER	Don't concern yourself about that.
DR. PIOUK	All right, all right, I am listening.
GLAZIER	Within a viewpoint that is not the same as yours, far from it. Whether he gets a new lease on life, as you put it so prettily, or goes on wallowing here or whether he croaks, it is completely one and the same to me, provided that the thing is not groundless, understand?
DR. PIOUK	I admit —
GLAZIER	You need reasons, God damn it! Why has he given up everything? Why this senseless existence? Why consent to die? Reasons! Jesus himself had his reasons. Whatever he does, it has to be known more or less why. Otherwise he is going to be spewed out. And the rest of us with him. Whom do you think we are dealing with? With esthetes?
DR. PIOUK	I don't get you and no mistake.
GLAZIER	Don't you see that we are all busy focusing over and over on something that has no meaning? A meaning for it must be found,

otherwise we might as well ring down the curtain.

DR. PIOUK   So what? I have no objection to the curtain's being rung down on something senseless, besides, that's what most often happens. In any case, I see that for you that's not the point. I will therefore not insist. I want quite simply to reply. You want to impose on this — how shall I put it — this semblance of a life a manner of justification, so that both the one leading it and those it grieves may, in your oh so pretty phrase, be put up with. That's more or less it? Good. That's what I do when I'm presenting the interested party with the possibility of taking his refusal as far as it will go in the neatest and nicest way imaginable. For it is very much a question of a refusal, if I understood it correctly.

GLAZIER   Yes. But you reason like a swine.

DR. PIOUK   It is so you may follow me better. Let's see. I offer him (He pats his vest) my little candy bar. He refuses. All right. Why? No matter. He wants to live. That's enough. It is a meaning. A little vague, if you like, but sufficient. People tell each other — I am poaching on

your preserves — The poor young
man! So near giving away! Saw the
light at the last minute! At the
very edge of the abyss! One of
ours once more! They won't ask
for anything more, believe me. Or
then again, he accepts. Meaning?
He has had enough. Why? Of no
importance whatsoever. He wants
to die. That's enough. It's clear.
It's luminous. Existence so weighs
him down that he prefers to
cancel himself out of it. Everybody
understands that. It's no longer
the Third Republic. No need to
come up with chancres. And there
you have it. It's as uncomplicated
as that. (To Olga) Coming?

GLAZIER   You do have a way of simplifying
                   things!

DR. PIOUK   Everything aspires to be either
                   black or white. Color is the miss-
                   ing of a beat. (Prestidigitator's
                   gesture, after the bringing off of a
                   sleight of hand)

MLLE. SKUNK   But is he going to come back
                   here?

DR. PIOUK   Here or elsewhere, little does it
                   matter.

MLLE. SKUNK   But he won't let you in! He won't
                   listen to you! He won't answer
                   you!

DR. PIOUK	(Laughing) You don't know me. (Pause) Not yet. (To the Glazier) Good night. (He leads Mlle. Skunk away)
GLAZIER	You will come tomorrow?
DR. PIOUK	(Halting) The earlier the better. (He takes out his memorandum-book and flips through it) Let's see — tonight — tonight I have an engagement — tomorrow — tomorrow - we have the funeral — funeral — lunch at the widow's — reading of the will — let's see — tomorrow afternoon, around three o'clock, three-thirty. (Makes a note) All right with you?
MLLE. SKUNK	And if he isn't here.
DR. PIOUK	Well then — well — then we shall see. And on that note. (To the Glazier) Goodnight.
MLLE. SKUNK	Goodnight. (Exit Mlle. Skunk and Dr. Piouk. A silence. The Glazier sits down on the bed, takes his head in his hands. Michel emerges from the shadows and goes and stands in front of him)
MICHEL	(Holding the sandwich) Eat your *tartine*, papa.
GLAZIER	(Lifting his head) Ah yes. (He takes the sandwich) You call that a *tartine*? (He separates the two

slices) Here we have a *tartine*,
Michel. And here is another. (He
puts them back together) And
here we have a sandwich. You
understand?

MICHEL   Yes, papa.

GLAZIER   (His mouth full) A sandwich, it's
two *tartines* stuck together. (A
silence) Repeat.

MICHEL   A sandwich is two *tartines* stuck
together.

GLAZIER   Good. (A silence. The Glazier
reflects) By the way, Michel.

MICHEL   Yes, papa.

GLAZIER   Are you happy with me?

MICHEL   What is it, happy, papa?

GLAZIER   How old are you?

MICHEL   Ten years old, papa.

GLAZIER   Ten years old. (A silence) And you
don't know what that means,
happy?

MICHEL   No, papa.

GLAZIER   You know when there is something that pleases you. It's a good
feeling, isn't it?

MICHEL   Yes, papa.

GLAZIER   Well then, happy is pretty much
that. (A silence) So, are you
happy?

MICHEL   No, papa.

GLAZIER   And why is that?

MICHEL	I don't know, papa.
GLAZIER	It's because you don't go to school enough?
MICHEL	No, papa, I don't like school.
GLAZIER	You would like to play with your little buddies.
MICHEL	No, papa, I don't like to play.
GLAZIER	I'm not mean to you?
MICHEL	Oh no, papa.
GLAZIER	What do you like to do?
MICHEL	I don't know.
GLAZIER	What do you mean, you don't know? Something has to be the matter.
MICHEL	(Upon reflection) I like when I am in bed, before I go to sleep.
GLAZIER	And why is that?
MICHEL	I don't know, papa. (A silence)
GLAZIER	Make the most of it.
MICHEL	Yes, papa. (A silence)
GLAZIER	Come, let me give you a kiss. (Michel moves forward. The Glazier kisses him) You like when I kiss you?
MICHEL	Not very much, papa.
GLAZIER	And why is that?
MICHEL	It prickles, papa?
GLAZIER	You see, you do know why you

	don't like when I kiss you.
MICHEL	Yes, papa.
GLAZIER	Then say why you like when you are in bed.
MICHEL	(Upon reflection) I don't know, papa. (A silence)
GLAZIER	You are still hungry.
MICHEL	Yes, papa.
GLAZIER	(Giving him the sandwich) Here, eat that.
MICHEL	(Hesitating) But it's yours, papa.
GLAZIER	(Forcefully) Eat! (A silence)
MICHEL	You aren't hungry any more, papa?
GLAZIER	No.
MICHEL	And why is that? (A silence)
GLAZIER	I don't know, Michel. (A silence)

CURTAIN

ACT III

The next day. Late afternoon.

Victor's room seen from another angle. Krap family side swallowed up by the pit.

Door ajar, windowpane broken, Glazier's tools in disorder on the floor.

Victor alone, in bed. He is sleeping. The Glazier in the doorway.

VICTOR (In his sleep) No — no — too high — rocks — my body — papa — be brave — good little boy — I am brave — a good little boy — good little boy. (A silence. He tosses and turns. Louder) Fathom — full fathom five — at low tide — low water — deep — deep — deep surge. (A silence. Enter the Glazier. He goes toward the bed) There the eyes — a thousand ships — the towers — circumcised — fire — fire.
(A silence)

GLAZIER The towers circumcised fire fire! Boy! Nice touch! (He shakes Victor) Up, sump! (Victor awakens with a start, sits up, haggard)

VICTOR (Half-awake) No — no — tomorrow I — (He sees the Glazier) What?

GLAZIER	A little past four! Four o'clock! Day is done. The sun is setting. Your father is in his grave. And here you are wallowing in your lustful dreams! Swine!
VICTOR	I am thirsty.
GLAZIER	(Pulling back the covers) Get up, God damn it! You are having callers.
VICTOR	(He sits at the edge of the bed. Dressed like the night before, but without his suit jacket) I'm incredibly thirsty. (He wipes his mouth) Callers?
GLAZIER	A good thing I stopped by. They would have found you snoring away.
VICTOR	Who? Who would have found me?
GLAZIER	Ah, here we go!
VICTOR	I am leaving. (He gets up, starts searching)
GLAZIER	Let us say it's an arraignment by proxy. Today is the third day, the great day, when everything is to be cleared up. In an hour we will know where we stand. What are you looking for?
VICTOR	The glass.
GLAZIER	The glass? Here. That's a good one.
VICTOR	(Searching) I saw it the other day.

(He looks under the bed, sees the glass, picks it up, goes out on the landing, comes back with the glass full of water, sits down on the bed, empties the glass in one gulp, waits, goes back out on the landing, comes back with the glass full again, empties it again, in two gos, places it on the bed, gets up, searches)

GLAZIER It's a family vault you have?

VICTOR (Searching) What?

GLAZIER Fashionable folks like you, there has got to be a family vault.

VICTOR The grain of wheat discovered in a hypogeum is sprouting after three thousand years of dry sleep. (Pause) So they say. (He searches) (A silence)

GLAZIER What's the matter that you're floundering around like — like a lost soul?

VICTOR I am looking for my shoes.

GLAZIER (Also searching, after a while) Here is one. (He kicks it toward Victor who sticks his foot into it) You're thinking of going out?

VICTOR (Searching) And the other one?

GLAZIER (He goes to shut the door and leans back against it) You will not be going out.

VICTOR I had it last night.

(A knock)

GLAZIER	There they are. (He opens the door. Enter Jacques, a shoe in his hand. He looks at the Glazier with astonishment, wants to speak to him, changes his mind, moves forward in the room)
JACQUES	I hope I am not disturbing Monsieur.
VICTOR	(Looking at the shoe) Where did you find that?
JACQUES	On the staircase, Monsieur. I thought I recognized Monsieur's shoe. (He proffers the shoe to Victor who takes it, examines it, drops it and sticks his foot in it)
GLAZIER	A flunkey!
VICTOR	It's you who's the caller? (Jacques uncomprehending)
GLAZIER	With all due respect to Monsieur, no, it is not he who is Monsieur's caller.
JACQUES	Monsieur is expecting a caller?
VICTOR	No, I am going out.
JACQUES	Monsieur got back all right?
VICTOR	I don't know. (He starts searching again)
JACQUES	Monsieur is looking for something?
VICTOR	My jacket. (Jacques helps him look for the jacket) I lost it. (He

goes toward the door)

JACQUES	Monsieur is not going to go out with no jacket!
VICTOR	(To the Glazier) Let me through.
GLAZIER	No.
VICTOR	(To Jacques) Help me get out.
JACQUES	Monsieur cannot get out?
VICTOR	He is not letting me through.
JACQUES	(Getting closer to the door) What am I to do, Monsieur?
VICTOR	Force him to let me through.
JACQUES	(Stepping forward, to the Glazier) Get yourself away from there. (The Glazier pushes him away violently. Jacques staggers back a few steps, stops)
VICTOR	(To Jacques) Both of us together.
JACQUES	(Unenthusiastically) Just as Monsieur wishes. (He moves forward)
GLAZIER	Stop! (Jacques stops) You loved your master?
VICTOR	Don't listen to him. Come on, together now.
GLAZIER	He loved his son?
JACQUES	(Wanting to satisfy everybody) Is that any of your concern?
VICTOR	(Slackly) So. One, two —
GLAZIER	(To Jacques, forcefully) He has to stay here. For his own good. (Pause) Furthermore I won't hesitate to knock both of you out

cold. (A silence. Victor goes and sits down on the bed. Jacques ill at ease)

JACQUES   Monsieur is angry? (A silence) I am embarrassed, Monsieur. Violence, it's not my cup of tea, Monsieur. I beg Monsieur's pardon.

VICTOR   Of course, of course. (Pause) What do you want?

JACQUES   I had something to tell Monsieur. (Pause) I haven't been sent. I thought —

VICTOR   Say it.

JACQUES   Madame, Monsieur's mother —

GLAZIER   Is this formality absolutely necessary?

VICTOR   He is right. Try to speak as if you were one human being and as if I myself were another. If you don't mind.

JACQUES   Monsieur, your mother is ill. The funeral is being postponed.

VICTOR   Two birds with one stone.

JACQUES   (Faintly scandalized) The funeral is set for tomorrow, Monsieur, the very last put-off date.

VICTOR   Then it's not that.

JACQUES   I thought it was necessary that you be forewarned, Monsieur. Madame is very low.

VICTOR	That is all?
JACQUES	No, Monsieur. Dr. Piouk had an attack during the night. He is confined to his bed.
GLAZIER	Shit!
VICTOR	Dr. who?
JACQUES	Dr. Piouk, Monsieur, the husband of Madame your aunt, Monsieur.
VICTOR	The husband of my aunt?
GLAZIER	But of course, the husband of your aunt. (To Jacques) What's the matter with him?
JACQUES	I do not know exactly.
GLAZIER	Is it very serious?
JACQUES	I believe that it is quite serious.
VICTOR	And it's for that you have come? To tell me that my mother is very low and that the husband of my aunt, whom I believed was a virgin, has had an attack during the night?
GLAZIER	Why, isn't he chatty today!
JACQUES	I thought Monsieur should know —
GLAZIER	Whoa!
JACQUES	That you should know how things stand with your family, on this the eve of the funeral.
GLAZIER	He doesn't give a tinker's damn.
JACQUES	And besides I wanted to make sure that Monsieur — that you had gotten back all right last night

	and then to tell you how happy those words of yours have made us, Marie and me.
Glazier	Words? He has been wording?
Jacques	I am perhaps being impertinent, but it has never been the same house since you left, Monsieur Victor. We were not told anything, naturally, but we knew enough to get an idea of the life you were leading (Circling look) A faint idea. We — I am not boring you Monsieur? (A silence) I am boring you, I knew it.
Glazier	It doesn't matter. Go on.
Jacques	I may go on, Monsieur?
Victor	(To the Glazier) You will let me through?
Glazier	Get this straight. I ask only one thing, that you take shape. The faintest glimmer of sense, enough to make people say, Ah, it's that, now I am beginning to under- stand, and I vanish.
Victor	(To Jacques) Go on.
Jacques	I don't quite know how to say it. I was only wishing that you knew —
Glazier	Might have known.
Jacques	How touched we have been, Marie and me, by what you told us. We would have liked to tell you last night, but you left so abruptly.

GLAZIER	Patience, patience.
JACQUES	We had so often asked ourselves what had happened, why you never came to the house. It distressed us to see Monsieur so sad. We didn't want to think badly of you, you had been so good to us, and yet there were times when — So it gave us quite a turn when you explained —
GLAZIER	Explained? What did he explain?
JACQUES	(Spluttering) Why — he explained to us — he told us why — why he couldn't do otherwise.
GLAZIER	He explained that to you?
JACQUES	Yes.
GLAZIER	And you understood? (Jacques embarrassed) You haven't understood a thing.
JACQUES	That is to say —
GLAZIER	You recall what he said?
JACQUES	We understood that it was serious, that it wasn't —
GLAZIER	I am asking you to repeat a sentence for me, one whole sentence. (A silence) This is first-rate, it's not enough that he insists on explaining himself only in the wings, but he requires imbeciles to the bargain.
JACQUES	It was clear at the time. It isn't something you can talk about. It's

a little like music.

GLAZIER   Music! (He walks back and forth in front of the door) How many crimes! How many crimes! (He halts) Music! I see it from here. Life, death, freedom, the whole kit and caboodle, and the disillusioned little laughs to show they are not taken in by the big words and the bottomless silences and the paralytic's gestures to signal that that's not it, they say that but that's not it, it's a different matter, an altogether different matter, what can you do, language isn't made to express those things. So let's keep quiet, decency, a little decency, goodnight, let's get to bed, we who senselessly dared to speak of something other than staple rationing. Ah, I hear it, your music. You were all plastered, naturally.

JACQUES   Plastered?

GLAZIER   He speaks! It's music. You listen to him. You understand. You no longer understand. He loses his shoes. He loses his jacket. At four in the afternoon he is still snoring. He's raving. The towers — circumcised — fire — fire. You come to see if he got back all right. It's clear. (To Victor) I bet you don't recall a word you said.

VICTOR	What? I can leave now?
GLAZIER	You see this character?
VICTOR	I don't understand.
GLAZIER	He's a domestic.
VICTOR	Well, I know him.
GLAZIER	He purposely takes the trouble to thank you for the revelations that you were nice enough to make last night, to him and to someone by the name of Marie. That, you've understood?
VICTOR	Revelations? (To Jacques) I made revelations to you?
GLAZIER	Call it what you like. What did you tell him?
VICTOR	Why — I don't recall exactly. It was of no interest.
GLAZIER	Music of no interest. You were all plastered, I am telling you.
JACQUES	I assure you that —
GLAZIER	You don't know these exceptional temperaments. One look at a cork and they are out of commission. You're not going to make me believe he could confront his papa's remains without the aid of a stimulant.
VICTOR	Don't you be concerning yourself about my father.
GLAZIER	(Rubbing his hands) Ah, that's

how we'll get him!

AUDIENCE MEMBER (Standing up in a stage-box) Stop! (He straddles stiffly the side of the stage-box and comes down cautiously onto the stage. He advances toward the bed) I am sorry for this intrusion.

GLAZIER You've been elected?

AUDIENCE MEMBER No, not precisely. But I've been at the bar, in the lobby, and I have been chatting with relatives, friends. I even came across a critic, at the first intermission.

GLAZIER Was he on his way in or on his way out?

AUDIENCE MEMBER He was on his way out.

GLAZIER In a word, you've been seeing which way the wind lies.

AUDIENCE MEMBER There you go!

GLAZIER And it's what has blown you in.

AUDIENCE MEMBER If you like. But basically I had just to listen to myself. For I am not one audience member, but a thousand, all slightly different from each other. I've always been like that, like an old blotter, of extremely variable porosity.

GLAZIER You can't be one to get bored silly.

AUDIENCE MEMBER (With high seriousness) Actually, yes, it can happen.

GLAZIER And you have always been like

that, like an old blotter?

AUDIENCE MEMBER Monsieur, when I was a baby my
mother would sometimes deny me
the breast, doubtless deeming that
I was overindulging. Well, I saw
her point!

(Enter Madame Karl)

MME. KARL   I've had enough.

GLAZIER   Me too.

MME. KARL   (Advancing toward the bed, to
Victor) For the la —
(She sees the Audience member)
Who is this one here?

GLAZIER   It is the people's commissary.

MME. KARL   I didn't see him go by.

GLAZIER   He came through the roof.

MME. KARL   (To the Glazier) You think you're
hot stuff, don't you?

GLAZIER   Stuff? What stuff, Madame? What
is this new insinuation?

MME. KARL   Ah! (Gesture of disgust, to Victor)
For the last time, are you staying
or are you leaving?

VICTOR   What?

MME. KARL   (Violently) I am asking you if you
are staying or if you are leaving.
I've had a bellyful.

GLAZIER   You're not the only one.

VICTOR   If I am staying or if I am leaving.
(He reflects) You want to know if I
am staying or if I am leaving?

GLAZIER	That's not it, you haven't understood. She wants —
MME. KARL	(To the Glazier) Shut up! (To Victor) Yesterday you were leaving, then you were no longer leaving, this morning you were still leaving, yet here you are. You have the bill. Pay me and beat it. I have two blokes after the room.
VICTOR	You cannot drive me out like that.
MME. KARL	Drive you out! You were the one asking to leave!
VICTOR	I believe I made a mistake.
GLAZIER	And besides what do you mean by this kind of behavior? Don't you see we are in conference? It is a historic moment and you come and pester us with your running on about some furnished room.
MME. KARL	You know what you can do with your conferences.
VICTOR	Listen, Madame Karl, I am going out in a little while — (He falls into a reverie)
MME. KARL	You know —
GLAZIER	Shush! He is meditating. (A silence)
VICTOR	I am going out for some fresh air.
GLAZIER	What poetry! What profundity!
VICTOR	I will tell you on my way out what I've decided.

MME. KARL	And then on your way back you'll tell me that you changed your mind.
VICTOR	No, Madame Karl, it will be a firm decision, I promise you.
MME. KARL	Because I've had just about enough.
GLAZIER	And what do you think I've had?
MME. KARL	Up to here. (She indicates the level. Exit) (A silence)
AUDIENCE MEMBER	That woman is right. (Pause) What was I saying? Oh yes, my mother, yes —
STAGE-BOX VOICE	Enough blabbering! Cut to the chase!
GLAZIER	Better you, obviously, than rotten eggs.
AUDIENCE MEMBER	I promise nothing. (Takes out his watch) Ten-thirty. Which means this has been going on for an hour and a half. (He puts back his watch. To Victor) Can you imagine?
VICTOR	What?
GLAZIER	Don't make things worse.
AUDIENCE MEMBER	You are right. I will try to stay calm. And to act quickly. For time (He takes out his watch) is a-wasting. (He puts back his watch) Sit down.

Glazier	Sit down?
Audience member	Why, yes. We are all sick and tired of seeing you float about like leaves, in the void.
Glazier	But where?
Audience member	On the floor, on the bed, wher-ever you like.
Glazier	(To Jacques) Well, my friend, what do you say to that?
Jacques	I must go.
Audience member	(Vehemently) Sit down! (Jacques and the Glazier, the latter with feigned eagerness, sit on the bed, one on either side of Victor who has sunk back on his elbow and whom the Glazier roughly sits back up straight. The Audience member turns around toward the stage-box) Hand me a chair, Maurice. (A chair is handed to him) And my coat. (His coat is handed to him. He brings the chair in front of the bed, puts on his coat, sits down, crosses his legs, runs his hand through his thin-ning hair, gets up again, goes back under the stage-box) And my hat. (His hat is handed to him, he puts it on and goes back and sits down)
Glazier	I forgot my scratch-pad. .
Audience member	I will be brief. Interrupt only if you are sure you can show off

your cleverness. We've had to go a
bit without up to now. (He clears
his throat) There. I'll try to stay
within the bounds of good taste.
This farce has — but I was forget-
ting. Before we start (to the Glazier), where is your son today?

GLAZIER   He is sick.

AUDIENCE MEMBER   Here we have an answer worthy of
this production. I am not asking
you how he is, I am asking you
WHERE HE IS.

GLAZIER   He is at home, in bed.

AUDIENCE MEMBER   And the mother?

GLAZIER   (Threateningly) Don't you be
concerning yourself about the
mother.

AUDIENCE MEMBER   All right, all right, that's all we
wanted to know.

GLAZIER   Fortunately for you.

AUDIENCE MEMBER   All right. This farce — (He again
clears his throat, but this time,
instead of swallowing the result,
he expels it into his handker-
chief) — this farce has gone on
long enough.

GLAZIER   My very own words.

AUDIENCE MEMBER   I say farce intentionally, in the
hope of covering for you. That's
what is done by our best authors,
labelling their most serious works
in this way in case they can't

	possibly be taken seriously.
STAGE-BOX VOICE	No more farting around! The chase, the chase.
AUDIENCE MEMBER	It's odd. No sooner among you, on the boards, than I start losing my grip. (Pause) A by no means inconsiderable one. (Pause) Everything is becoming hazy, vague, and I can no longer make heads or tails out of it. (Puts his hand before his eyes) I don't even know any more what I was saying.
STAGE-BOX VOICE	The play's the thing! Enough already. (The prompter emerges from his box, climbs up on the stage, the script in his hand)
PROMPTER	That's it! All over! You are not following the script. You make me sick. Goodnight. (Exit)
GLAZIER	The script! The script! Leave the script with us! (Enter the script by air. It crashes to earth) We're really in for it now!
AUDIENCE MEMBER	I am going to make one last effort.
GLAZIER	Just a minute! (To Jacques and Victor) What are you muttering for like that? (They go silent. To the Audience member) What do you expect me to do with a guy like that?

AUDIENCE MEMBER	Let me fill you in. Now it's all coming back to me. This farce —
GLAZIER	But you don't need to repeat the same thing ten times. You're not in the lavatory any more, with the critics. Next. Next.
AUDIENCE MEMBER	You're wrong to go back over the critics. They can't bear more than one kick per play. It's not like cuckolds.
GLAZIER	Say what you have to say and let's have done with it.
AUDIENCE MEMBER	I notice one thing, I didn't leave. Why? Out of curiosity? If you like. For I am in part vile, by definition. To see whether you're going to be able to make him speak? If you like. To witness your absurd poisoning scene? I admit it, I am as much your village gossip as the gentleman who doesn't get taken in. And besides my friend's wife is free only after eleven o'clock and for all that it's a little warmer here than in the cafe. (He shivers, turns up his coat-collar) But all that isn't much. No, if I'm still here it's that there is something in this business that literally paralyzes me and leaves me completely dumbfounded. How do you explain that? You play chess? No. It doesn't matter. It's like when

you watch a chess game between players of the lowest class. For three quarters of an hour they haven't touched a single piece. They sit there gaping at the board like two horses' asses and you're also there, even more of a horse's ass than they are, nailed to the spot, disgusted, bored, worn-out, filled with wonder at so much stupidity. Up until the moment when you can't take it anymore. Then you tell them, So do that, do that, what are you waiting for, do that and it's all over, we can go to bed. It's inexcusable, it goes against the most elementary know-how, you haven't even met the guys, but it's stronger than you, it's either that or a fit. There you have pretty much what's happening to me. *Mutatis mutandis,* of course. You get me?

GLAZIER   No. We are not playing chess.

AUDIENCE MEMBER   It's this servant business that has done us in. Your comic, what do you call him — (He consults his program) — Victor, he makes a pretense of wanting to speak to us and then into the wings he goes to tell his paltry little tales to some numbskull flunkey. No, no, there's a limit.

GLAZIER	(To Jacques) You put up with being treated in this way?
JACQUES	You need a manservant. Allow him to have the soul of one.
GLAZIER	Wham! (He covers his eye)
AUDIENCE MEMBER	Such a lack of awareness —
GLAZIER	Ultimately you are tiresome, you are truly tiresome. You understand nothing of what's going on. You get here all frolicking and rollicking, your pockets stuffed full of solutions. But which ones? For ten minutes you've been chewing our ear off and we're still waiting. Aside from your chess story, which doesn't hang together, you still haven't said anything that I myself haven't already said a hundred times over, and much better. You're disturbing us, that's all. You think he's going to confide in you? Of course not, you're hateful to him, one more pain in the ass, no more, no less. (He gets up, suddenly furious) But what did you come here to do? Just when I was in the midst of worming his secrets out of him! Just when everything was going to work out! (He moves forward) Get the hell out of here! Get the hell out! (He turns around at the sound of

	Victor getting up and clumsily springing toward the door. The Glazier makes a headlong dash, catches Victor, lands him a slap, leads him back to the bed, forces him to sit down. To Victor) Bastard! (He raises his hand. Victor shrivels up)
AUDIENCE MEMBER	Oh boy, oh boy, oh boy! Not like that! Not like that!
GLAZIER	I'm giving you the floor for the last time. Then I'm booting you into the pit, with a kick in the ass, in your thousand asses. Gladly! Gladly!
AUDIENCE MEMBER	That would be to let all hell break loose.
GLAZIER	Well then, I'll let it break loose, hell, I mean. That will still be better than your bleating like a — like a season-ticket holder! (He bends raging over Victor and shakes him) Vermin! Son of a bitch! Will you speak at last? Speak! (He lets him go all of a sudden, collapsing on the bed) Victor! (He takes his head in his hands)
AUDIENCE MEMBER	(He returns to his chair, leans with his fingertips against its back in an elegant stance) I will be brief. I make out, in this racket, two stances confronting each

other. I make them out dimly but I do make them out. First (To the Glazier) yours. About which I cannot tell if it is moral, esthetic, intellectual or whether it doesn't stem quite simply from a kind of taylorizing sentimentality, so vague and entangled are your references. And then that, much simpler, of Dr. — (He consults his program) — Dr. Piouk, who seems to believe, in so far as he knows French, that one turns away from pain as necessarily and, let's be fair, with as much blindness as the butterfly from the darkness. I say confronting each other, but they don't even confront each other. Set forth with vagueness, with weariness, they coexist, if you can call that coexisting, six of one and half a dozen of the other, so little does anybody give a damn. And it's with that you are laying claim to making this unfortunate (Program) — this unfortunate Victor a figure of farce. (He wipes his forehead) But that's just the tip of the iceberg. The awful thing is that all the time you graze something, oh I'm not saying it's important, but it could nonetheless make for our spending a halfway decent evening. There's a grazing, a grazing, and never a touching, it's terrible. (Pause) By the way, who put together this flop? (Program) Beckett (he says Béquet), Samuel, Béquet, Béquet, that's got to be a Jew from Greenland crossed with an Auvergnat.

GLAZIER　Don't know. Appears that he eats his soup with a fork.

AUDIENCE MEMBER　No matter. Pulp it. No, but seriously, this could have been really something. Imagine it with clear-headed types, fresh-sounding mouthpieces, the two ways of life, the two mainsprings, faith and pleasure, faith in anything at all and the least displeasure, and the unfortunate who wants neither one nor the other and who goes to rack and ruin looking for something different. I mean, there we would have had ourselves a good laugh. Well then, go to hell.

GLAZIER　You like states of affairs that are straightforward and clear-cut, preposterous and side-splitting.

AUDIENCE MEMBER　And what about you?

GLAZIER　Oh me, you know, I'm somebody who doesn't ask for a lot anymore. My requirements are shrinking by

the minute. The merest
streetlamp, just something to set
off the fog, and I'll go happy back
to nothingness.

AUDIENCE MEMBER Listen. Let's drop the subject of
what isn't and cannot be, unless
we take everything from the very
beginning. Let's view things as
they are. You want —

GLAZIER Let's view things as they are! But
where have you been all your life?
On the Canebière?

AUDIENCE MEMBER You want him to speak, yes or no?

GLAZIER Well! that's an idea. I hadn't
thought of that.

AUDIENCE MEMBER Let him tell us a little of what he
told that would-be music buff.
What do you think of that?

GLAZIER Why, that's an idea of genius. (He
turns politely toward Victor, lifting
his beret) Excuse me, Monsieur.
(He taps his shoulder) Excuse me,
Monsieur, forgive me for inter-
rupting your conversation, but if
you could summarize for us last
night's pronouncements, made in
the wings, under the sway of
alcohol, you would be doing us a
supremely good turn. (Attitude
increasingly humble and coaxing)
A whopping good turn!

AUDIENCE MEMBER You're going about it like an ass.

GLAZIER   (Going down on his knees, join-
                 ing his hands) Monsieur! Mon-
                 sieur! I entreat you! Have pity,
                 have pity for those who crawl
                 around in the darkness. (He
                 makes a show of giving ear)
                 Quiet! You'd think it was Pascal's
                 space. (He gets up dejectedly,
                 dusts off the knees of his trousers.
                 To the Audience member) You
                 see. (He reflects) I'm leaving.
                 You're taking my place, aren't
                 you? Here with him, here (Ges-
                 ture toward the audience) with
                 them. Thanks in advance.

AUDIENCE MEMBER Why, you're mad! Is it possible
                 you've forgotten? Or that you
                 haven't noticed? A thing that's
                 right before your very eyes!

GLAZIER   I am going back home, to
                 Crèvecoeur-sur-Auge. Goodnight,
                 everybody. (He goes)

AUDIENCE MEMBER (So forcefully that he coughs) He
                 is afraid of pain! (The Glazier
                 turns around. Coughing fits) It's
                 you he said it to! Imbecile! The
                 sole assertion that escaped him!

GLAZIER   You're exaggerating.

AUDIENCE MEMBER His one and only mistake — and
                 you don't take advantage of it!
                 (He coughs frenziedly)

GLAZIER   Something went down the wrong

way?

AUDIENCE MEMBER (Calming down) You'll be telling me that it's no longer any use, that it's too late, that we've lost the match. It's possible. It doesn't matter. It's all you have left, at the point you're at. You'll be telling me that what's said under duress has no value whatsoever as evidence. But it does, it does, whatever one says, one gives oneself away.

(Mme. Piouk rushes in)

MME. PIOUK André! André! (Jacques gets up) My husband. You haven't seen my husband?

GLAZIER (To the Audience member) You haven't seen her husband? No? Me neither. (He looks under the bed) He isn't here, Madame.

MME. PIOUK He didn't come!

AUDIENCE MEMBER Why, no, Madame. We were expecting him, even with a certain eagerness, and then we were told that he'd had an attack during the night. Of the liver, no doubt...? At any rate, it matters little. An attack of one sort or another. During the night. So we concluded from this that he would not be keeping his appointment. (To the Glazier) Am I right?

GLAZIER	I followed the exact same line of reasoning.
MME. PIOUK	Yes, indeed. He is very ill. He had to stay in bed, with ice packs, on his forehead and on his — his stomach. I left the room for a moment — (She wrings her hands) — miserable creature that I am, but I couldn't do otherwise, and when I went back in he wasn't there anymore! He'd gotten away! Half-undressed! With no hat! (Sobs) André! With no hat! I knew he was supposed to be coming here this afternoon. So I took a taxi. And he's not around!
GLAZIER	What a family!
AUDIENCE MEMBER	(Politely) But doubtless you've quite simply gotten here before him, Madame. Give him a little time. He won't be long.
MME. PIOUK	But he no longer knows what he's doing! It's dreadful!
AUDIENCE MEMBER	(Shocked) He no longer knows what he's doing?
GLAZIER	You've been to your sister's, Madame?
MME. PIOUK	Violette? No. Why? You believe he may have gone there?
GLAZIER	Seeing that he doesn't know what he's doing. (Pause) He perhaps wanted to ask after her.

MME. PIOUK	But he didn't even know — yes, he knew she was ill. I told him last night. But he must have forgotten. He'd forgotten everything. He no longer recognized me.
AUDIENCE MEMBER	If he has forgotten everything, the chances are slim that he'll be coming here. Stop and think a little, dear lady.
MME. PIOUK	But everything may have come back to him! All at once! (The Glazier's hysterical laughter. He goes back and forth with wayward gestures) What's to be done? (This passage comes abruptly to an end, as if overrun with a feeling of fatigue and fatuity. A silence. Gestures of helplessness, of indifference, shrugs. Even Jacques who has been within an inch of saying, What if Madame were to notify the police?, lifts up his arms and drops them listlessly. Mme. Piouk completely overcome. She goes to the door, hesitates, turns around, wants to speak, changes her mind, exits. Foreboding that the entire play could come to an end in the same way)
JACQUES	Let me go.
GLAZIER	(To the Audience member) Does anybody need him anymore?
AUDIENCE MEMBER	I don't.

GLAZIER	(To Jacques) Then you may go.
JACQUES	(To Victor) Monsieur does not wish for anything?
GLAZIER	Go, go, go. Monsieur is without wishes. Buzz off. (Jacques hesitates, looks at Victor with sadness, lifts up his arms, exits)
AUDIENCE MEMBER	Come on. One last effort.
GLAZIER	You think so?
VICTOR	I am thirsty.
AUDIENCE MEMBER	What did he say.
GLAZIER	That he's thirsty. (Pause) I don't know where we were anymore. All these interruptions...
AUDIENCE MEMBER	He fears pain.
GLAZIER	Ah yes. Maybe he was lying.
AUDIENCE MEMBER	We're going to find out.
GLAZIER	He can't be tortured.
AUDIENCE MEMBER	Why not?
GLAZIER	It isn't done.
AUDIENCE MEMBER	Since when?
GLAZIER	I couldn't.
AUDIENCE MEMBER	Me neither.
GLAZIER	Well then?
AUDIENCE MEMBER	You'll find out. (He turns toward the stage-box) Tchoutchi! Come along. (Tchoutchi comes down onto the stage, steps forward with a broad oriental grin) You understand. (Dilatation of grin) You have the pincers. (Tchoutchi

	displays the pincers. To the Glazier) Fill him in.
GLAZIER	Victor! (He shakes him) You must speak, right now.
VICTOR	What?
GLAZIER	You must explain yourself.
VICTOR	Explain what? I don't understand. Go away. (A gesture from the Audience member: Tchoutchi moves forward)
GLAZIER	(To the Audience member) He's Taoist?
AUDIENCE MEMBER	Unremittingly.
GLAZIER	Ow! (Tchoutchi moves forward) Victor! Wake up! This time it's serious. Your nails are going to be torn out. (To Tchoutchi) Isn't that so?
TCHOUTCHI	All flewll llnaills to llstarllt with.
GLAZIER	(To Victor) You hear? A few nails to start with.
	(Victor lifts his head, sees the Chinaman, smiles at him, pinches him, draws back in terror)
AUDIENCE MEMBER	He understands.
GLAZIER	(He keeps a strong hold on Victor) Speak! (Tchoutchi moves forward)
VICTOR	(Frantic) What? Speak of what? I don't know how to speak. What do you want from me? Murderers!

AUDIENCE MEMBER	(To the Glazier) Ask him some questions.
GLAZIER	Repeat what you said to Jacques.
VICTOR	But I didn't say anything to him! I don't know any more! I forget! What do you all have against me? I haven't done anything to you! Let me be!
AUDIENCE MEMBER	It's vague. Well, it's beginning to flow. (To Tchoutchi) By the way, you have the catheter? (Tchoutchi takes a broach out of his pocket and displays it. Grin)
GLAZIER	It is true that he hasn't done anything to us.
AUDIENCE MEMBER	His offense is not to have known how to hide. Ask him some questions.
GLAZIER	Why have you left your family? Your fiancée? Your amusements? Your labors? Why are you leading this life? What is your goal? What are your intentions?
VICTOR	I don't know, I don't know.
AUDIENCE MEMBER	You're asking him too many at a time.
GLAZIER	Why are you leading this life? No, it's not that. First, what is this life you've been leading, for more than two years? What —
AUDIENCE MEMBER	That will do. Tchoutchi. (Motions to him to move forward.

Tchoutchi moves forward. The Audience member as well. They stop in front of Victor) You heard the question? What is this life you're leading? (Pincer effects)

GLAZIER	Say something quick! Anything at all! We'll help you.
VICTOR	I'm going to try.
GLAZIER	Bravo! (To the Audience member and Tchoutchi) Stand back! Give him room to breathe. (The Audience member and Tchoutchi step back)
VICTOR	It won't be the truth.
GLAZIER	No importance whatsoever.
VICTOR	It'll be boring.
GLAZIER	Now that's far more serious.
VICTOR	You'll have only yourself to blame.
GLAZIER	Absolutely right. (A silence) Watch out! He's going to take the plunge.
VICTOR	When I was small —
AUDIENCE MEMBER	For pity's sake, no blow-by-blow accounts, our time is limited. Stick to the issue.
GLAZIER	Victor cut off! Now I've seen everything!
VICTOR	You find the way I live sordid and incomprehensible. It would be natural for you to turn away from it in disgust. But what do you do?

	You bear down on it, tirelessly. You can no longer break away. You go incessantly round and round. Nothing discourages you. And when night comes between us, you think about me.
Audience member	It's that you've entered the public domain.
Victor	I obsess you. Why? Sound your depths. It's not I whose depths should be sounded but your own.
Glazier	It's true that he doesn't know how to speak.
Victor	My family, my fiancée, my friends, maybe it's normal, what is called normal, for them to be sinking their teeth into me. But you? You're outsiders. I don't know you. What is it to you, how I live? And you are not the first. For as long as I've been living in this way, for two years, so you say, I've been a prey to strangers.
Glazier	People would like to understand. You provoke them.
Victor	But why this sudden rage to understand when it concerns a life like mine? Every day, calm and indifferent, you pass countless mysteries right by. And in front of me you stop, stricken, starving for consciousness, with your low

curiosity, dead set on seeing things in their true light. (A silence) Begrudgers! (A silence) The saints, the madmen, the martyresses, the death row inmates, that doesn't trouble you, it's within the order of things. They are outsiders, you will never be of their party, at least you hope so. You are not begrudging of them. You turn away from them. You don't want to think about it. They fill you with horror and pity. (A silence) Before the solution that's not the one that is death you are filled with horror and pity. With easiness as well. You're mind is set at rest. Not worth racking your brains. It's no business of yours. If from your misery they're a long way off, these folks, in another misery perhaps, but one not to be imagined, they have very much paid the price. So nothing's to be faulted. The books are balanced.

GLAZIER   What a jaw!

VICTOR   May I keep quiet now?

AUDIENCE MEMBER   Keep quiet! Why, you still haven't said anything useful. Get out a bit from under these generalities, if you please. We're preoccupied with your case, not with that of

	the human race.
Victor	But they are of a piece.
Audience member	What? Twaddle! And furthermore, speak a little louder, we can't hear you. (A silence) Hurry up!
Glazier	Give him time. It was the nightingale and not the lark.
Audience member	Time! Do you know what time it is. (He takes out his watch) Eleven o'clock. (He puts back his watch) And then some.
Glazier	You're six hours fast.
Audience member	Cut out the monkey business. He is being asked a clear and simple question: what is this life you're leading? And he answers with this hail of absurdities about our life, yours and mine, and that of asylum inmates. Let him answer the question, otherwise I take extreme measures.
Glazier	(To the Audience member) In a little while I'm going to bash your face in.
Victor	The life I'm leading? It's the one lived by he who wants no part of yours, oh I don't speak of yours personally, nobody would want any part of that, but of the life that is yours in the sense that between you and what they call the ones truly alive there is but a

difference of degree. But whether it's this superior way of life, or yours, or the others, I want no part of it, for I've taken it into my head that it's always a question of the same drudgery, at every rung of the ladder.

AUDIENCE MEMBER But you do live. You can't deny it. Where lies the difference between your life and ours? There is a difference apparently. But deep down?

VICTOR You really find that I live? You stoop to compare yourselves to me? With the worst beggar you may feel a kinship, but not with me. Would you be dead set on understanding me, on vindicating me, on getting me integrated, if you felt me deep down to be one of your own kind? No, for in that case there wouldn't be anything to understand. A pitying glance in passing, one of disgust, even of anger, and the matter would be settled, you would be thinking no more about it. But you feel there is something different, that my life is essentially other than yours, that between you and me there is a gap as there is a gap between you and the insane, only not the same gap. The plight of the insane, that

	you accept. Mine, no. Why? Unless I am insane as well. But you don't dare to hope so.
GLAZIER	Nothing bores like boredom.
AUDIENCE MEMBER	You're being asked what this life is you're leading. You've been instructing us as to everything it is not, sorry, I haven't annoyed you, I hope, as to a small part of what it is not. That's what's known as negative anthropology. You inform us on the same occasion of our feelings regarding you. We are better acquainted with them than you. If you are truly incapable of answering the question, say so, I'll see that you're given a hand.
VICTOR	It's a life —
AUDIENCE MEMBER	Sorry. One moment. You're speaking now of your very own life? Not of ours nor that of the bees?
VICTOR	Of mine.
AUDIENCE MEMBER	Capital.
VICTOR	It's a life eaten up by its freedom.
GLAZIER	What if we killed him? How would that do for curtains?
AUDIENCE MEMBER	Let's be patient a little longer. (To Victor) Go on.
VICTOR	It won't take a minute. I've always wanted to be free. I don't know why. Nor do I know what it means,

to be free. You could tear out all my fingernails and I still couldn't tell you. But far away from words I know what it is. I've always desired it. I still desire it. I desire only that. First I was the prisoner of others. So I left them. Then I was the prisoner of self. That was worse. So I left myself. (Wanders) (A silence)

AUDIENCE MEMBER But this is enthralling. How does one leave oneself?

VICTOR What?

AUDIENCE MEMBER I'm saying this is enthralling. Go on. Only tell us how one manages how to leave oneself.

VICTOR (Incoherently) You accept one's getting beyond life or its getting beyond you, one's becoming irreducible to it, on condition that the price is paid, that one's liberty is laid down. He abdicated, he died, he's mad, he has faith, a sarcoma, nothing to fault. But to be among you no longer through sheer plod of being free, now that's a disgrace and a scandal. So it's the old maid raging against the whore. This freedom of yours is so miserable! So scanty! So worn-out! So ugly! So false! And you set such store by it! It's all you talk about! Ah envious ones,

	envious ones! (Takes his head in his hands)
GLAZIER	Well what do you know, we've been set straight.
AUDIENCE MEMBER	Straight? About what? About us? (To Victor) Pull yourself together.
VICTOR	(Lifting his head) I have nothing more to tell you.
AUDIENCE MEMBER	But you do! you do! You have to tell us how you go about leaving yourself. This is of the most particular interest to my friends.
VICTOR	To hell with your friends.
AUDIENCE MEMBER	Tchoutchi. (Tchoutchi comes forward)
VICTOR	You can really put stock in what I say under duress? You're that hard up?
AUDIENCE MEMBER	We've already settled that question. In your absence. Besides, you have only to view the result. What you've said hangs together. It's a bit coarse-grained, a bit naive, but it does hang together. We ask no more. Our requirements are modest, contrary to what you seem to assume. (To the Glazier) Isn't that so?
GLAZIER	Leave me the hell alone.
AUDIENCE MEMBER	You left yourself. There we have the ultimate find among all your installments. How did you go

about it?

VICTOR   By being, as little as possible. By
                  not moving an inch, by not think-
                  ing, by not dreaming, by not
                  speaking, by not listening, by not
                  perceiving, by not knowing, by not
                  wanting, by not being able, and so
                  on and so forth. I believed that
                  was where my prisons lay.

GLAZIER   I believe I am going to throw up.

AUDIENCE MEMBER   Ah, so you believed. And you
                  managed, not to move an inch,
                  not to make a peep, and so on?
                  You must nevertheless have had a
                  bite from time to time, I assume,
                  during those two heroic years. It
                  must sometimes have been diffi-
                  cult to keep on being pure of all
                  ideation. And in your sleep you
                  did come forth, like an owl at
                  nightfall. To say nothing of the
                  visits inflicted upon you and
                  you're having had every now and
                  then to acquaint yourself with the
                  matter, in spite of yourself.

VICTOR   Patience is needed.

AUDIENCE MEMBER   Obviously, obviously, all begin-
                  nings are difficult. But for all that
                  you're already feeling a little less
                  — er — a little less captive?

VICTOR   I believe that it's the right track.

AUDIENCE MEMBER   And death plain and simple, that

	doesn't speak to you in any way?
VICTOR	If I was dead I wouldn't know I was dead. That's the only thing I've got against death. I want to squeeze pleasure out of my death. That's where freedom lies: seeing oneself dead. (A silence. The Glazier turns aside and hiccoughs into his handkerchief)
GLAZIER	(Wiping his mouth) I consider this discussion to be closed. The essential has been said.
AUDIENCE MEMBER	I am of your opinion. Everybody now has his little footing. To push things along any further would be to go back into the fog.
VICTOR	You know that what I told you isn't the truth.
AUDIENCE MEMBER	The truth! (To the Glazier) Did you hear him? He's in a class by himself! (To Victor) We know, Monsieur, we know, don't get all worked up about it. For the truth we apply elsewhere, everybody has his dealer. No, don't distress yourself on that score. Besides, you don't know what it is that's the truth. Nor do we. You perhaps spoke it without knowing it. And without our knowing it.
VICTOR	I told you a story so you would

leave me alone.

AUDIENCE MEMBER   If you like, if you like. Perhaps less
than you think. Stories, well
there's no getting them told with
impunity. In any event, you're not
being asked for more. It wasn't
bad at all, your story, a bit long, a
bit boring, a bit silly, but not bad,
not bad at all, even pretty-sound-
ing in spots, on condition that
one isn't too particular, something
we never are. I congratulate you, I
thank you and I excuse MYSELF.

VICTOR   I have something to add.

GLAZIER   He's insane. Give them a finger
and they take an arm.

AUDIENCE MEMBER   No, no, don't add anything,
you're going to botch everything,
believe me.

VICTOR   One word.

AUDIENCE MEMBER   (Magnanimously) All right then,
one word if you absolutely insist,
but no more.

VICTOR   I'm letting go.
(A silence)

AUDIENCE MEMBER   You are letting go?

GLAZIER   Don't do that, don't say that! Just
when everything is settled.

VICTOR   I'm giving up on being free. One
can't be free. I was mistaken. I
can't lead this life any more. I
understood that last night, in

	seeing my father. One cannot see oneself dead. It's theatrics. I no —
AUDIENCE MEMBER	Wait, wait, let me stop and think! (He reflects) This changes everything. (To the Glazier) What do you say to that?
GLAZIER	I say shit to that. (Pause) And shit again.
AUDIENCE MEMBER	After all, why not? It's perhaps better this way. (To Victor) And what do you intend to do in that case? What is there left for you to do?
VICTOR	I don't know.
GLAZIER	(Moaning) It's starting all over again.
AUDIENCE MEMBER	You can no longer stay like this?
VICTOR	No, I no longer can.
AUDIENCE MEMBER	It's overtaxing you?
VICTOR	Yes.
AUDIENCE MEMBER	Well then, be logical. It's either life, with all that it entails of — of subjection, or — the great leave-taking, the real one, to use an image you hold dear. No?
VICTOR	I don't know.
AUDIENCE MEMBER	Well, for crying out loud!
GLAZIER	He can drop dead now. We know why. Let's get out of here.
AUDIENCE MEMBER	Or he can return to his family, revive his mother, lay his father to

rest, come into his inheritance, gratify his fiancée's every whim, start up a magazine, a church, a home of his own, a movie club, and who knows what else? Living or dead, he belongs among us, again he's one of ours. That's all that had to be worked out. That basically there is only us. It's even much better this way. There's more decency in it. (To Victor) Thank you! (He moves forward, extending his hand) Brother! (Victor doesn't take his hand, perhaps hasn't seen it) No? It doesn't matter. Of no importance whatsoever. Simply a question of taste. Goodnight. Come, Tchoutchi. (He heads for the stage-box, followed by Tchoutchi, for all that still smiling)

GLAZIER   Through there. (He points to the wings)

AUDIENCE MEMBER   Why?

GLAZIER   Through there, I tell you. (He moves forward, threateningly. The Audience member faces up to him. Tchoutchi as well) You think I'm afraid of your Pekingese? (He moves forward)

AUDIENCE MEMBER   Your attitude amazes me. I bail you out and you threaten me with

	violence.
VICTOR	What difference can it possibly make which way he goes out? Now that the damage is done.
AUDIENCE MEMBER	The damage! That's how you thank me!
GLAZIER	Abortionist! Baboon! (He moves forward. The Audience member and Tchoutchi draw back toward the wing in question) Huckster! (The Audience member and Tchoutchi exit hastily. The Glazier takes the chair and hurls it after them, into the wing. Resounding crash) Bastard! (He goes toward Victor) He took us for a ride! (He sees the prompter's script on the floor, picks it up, throws it into the wing) Peace of filth! (He goes back and forth, furious. He stops in front of Victor) You couldn't have told that to us two hours — two years — ago? (Pause) Ham! (He resumes his walk) Still, what a put-on. (He stops before his tools scattered all over the floor, gazes upon them in disgust) Will you look at that!
VICTOR	Bawl me out a wee bit more.
GLAZIER	I don't have the heart to pick them up. (He moves the tools about with the tips of his toes) It would've been nice to take the

	diamond along with me. (He looks for it) So much the worse. (Victor gets up and goes to help him look for the diamond) What are you doing?
VICTOR	I'm looking for the diamond. (He moves the tools about with his foot) It's perhaps your son who has it.
GLAZIER	My son? You think so? It's possible.
VICTOR	He's not here.
GLAZIER	I don't know.
VICTOR	You're leaving the window like that?
GLAZIER	Yes.
VICTOR	And the door?
GLAZIER	I'm leaving it like that.
VICTOR	You're coming back tomorrow?
GLAZIER	No.
VICTOR	Then take your belongings.
GLAZIER	I'm giving them to you.
VICTOR	You've done some very fine work.
GLAZIER	Yes. (A silence) I shouldn't have waked you up. (Pause) You were dreaming?
VICTOR	Yes.
GLAZIER	What?
VICTOR	I was dreaming of my father. He was —
GLAZIER	No, no, don't say it. I hate the

firsthand accounts of dreams.

VICTOR   He was in the water and I myself was on the diving board. It was —

GLAZIER   Don't say it!

VICTOR   The sea was full of rocks. He told me to dive in.

GLAZIER   To dive in?

VICTOR   I myself didn't want to.

GLAZIER   And why was that?

VICTOR   I was afraid to get hurt. I was afraid of the rocks. I was afraid of drowning. I didn't know how to swim.

GLAZIER   He would have saved you.

VICTOR   That's what he told me.

GLAZIER   Still, you did dive in.
(A silence)

VICTOR   I have that dream all the time. (A silence) You knew that guy?

GLAZIER   Which guy? Oh, that one. Thousand-butts. (He reflects) My anger has died down. How did that happen?

VICTOR   Who's there?

GLAZIER   What? Oh yes. I don't know. *Manille*, billiards, plentiful fare painstakingly prepared, pain in the cecum, Saturday night lovemaking after the show, a weakness for clarity, nothing to excess — (He listens) There is somebody on the landing. (Gently he opens the door slightly, looks outside, a silence. He gently shuts the door) Well, of all things! (He rubs his hands) Now this is a real surprise. I'd never have expected it.

VICTOR   Who's there?

GLAZIER   It's the Catalysis King and his sweetheart. It will take them a minute. (He reflects) You don't want to see this piece of trash through to the bitter end?

VICTOR   I don't understand.

GLAZIER   Telling us what you've decided. (The door opens slightly, the Glazier rushes to shut it again. Through the door) One moment! We'll call you! Do go on pawing each other for a bit! While awaiting better things! (To Victor) Yes indeed, what you've decided on the horns of the dilemma Dupont.

VICTOR   I haven't decided anything.

GLAZIER   Except that you can't go on like this. So? One more little shake of the ass, Ducky. The last. Come one. Be nice.

VICTOR   I'm telling you I don't know. For you that's not enough of a slaughterfest?

GLAZIER   One tiny corpse more. What

	difference can it possibly make to you? Given the point you're at?
Victor	I don't know.
Glazier	I don't know, I don't know! Are you being asked to know? (The door opens again slightly, the Glazier shuts it again. Through the door) One moment! (To Victor) Say any old thing. You're coming in on the boogie-woogie, yes, or: shit, no? (Victor smiles) You're smiling? You dare to smile! (He opens the door. Enter Mlle. Skunk and Dr. Piouk, imperfectly attired)
Dr. Piouk	As mischievous as ever.
Mlle. Skunk	Victor! (She rushes into his arms. Unwieldy operation)
Glazier	(With butterflylike gestures) From flower to flower and from object to object.
Dr. Piouk	To work. My time is limited. Why do you remain in the gloom?
Glazier	Well, old bodice-basher, what's gotten into you? Your concubine has been looking everywhere for you.
Mlle. Skunk	(Moving away from the bed) He's in a sweat. (To the Glazier) You explained to him?
Dr. Piouk	Lights.
Glazier	How is his mother?

MLLE. SKUNK	Very ill. You told him?
GLAZIER	(To Victor) You hear? Mummy is at her last gasp. (Victor gets up, moves vaguely around the bed. Everyone looks at him in silence. He goes toward them) He lost his jacket.
DR. PIOUK	(Singing and dancing)

> *His trousers he did lose*
> *While dancing in his Charleston*
> *shoes.*

(Victor gives Mlle. Skunk a questioning look, indicating Dr. Piouk)

MLLE. SKUNK	Why, it's Marguerite's husband, for Pete's sake.
DR. PIOUK	Let me introduce myself: Dr. André Piouk, psychopath.
GLAZIER	And sociologist.
DR. PIOUK	At your service. Lights.
GLAZIER	Before we go any further —
DR. PIOUK	Lights.
GLAZIER	Just a minute, just a minute. Yes. I have a happy, a grand piece of news to announce to you. (Pause) There were many things happening here this afternoon. Astonishing things. What a pity you couldn't have witnessed them. But no doubt you had better things to do. (Pause) You recall last night's

pretty kettle of fish? Well, now
everything is in order, a little
parcel here, a little parcel there,
nicely tied, nicely labelled, a
mailman couldn't get it wrong. As
for your fiancé, Mademoiselle, he
was literally brilliant. He gave us
one of those presentations (gesture) fit for a board of directors. A
real treat. I have to say that we
were backed up, yes, by a sort of
outer-borough sub-Socrates.
Honor to whom honor. Without
him I don't know if we could have
brought it off. (To Victor) What
do you think?

MLLE. SKUNK   And the grand piece of news?

GLAZIER   Ah yes, the grand piece of news.
Well — brace yourselves — no, he
must tell you about that himself.
This moment is sacred. My lips
would defile it.

MLLE. SKUNK   (To Victor) Well?

VICTOR   You're still giving heed to this
joker?

GLAZIER   That's the thanks I get.

MLLE. SKUNK   Then it isn't true?

DR. PIOUK   I said to her, verbatim, Dear Olga,
my dear little Olga, do you want
me to help you? To get him back
for you? Safe and sound? Into
your pretty arms? Well! Dear Olga.

	(Pause) She got the point.
GLAZIER	(To Victor) You hear that? Her most precious possession! So that you might live! Monster!
DR. PIOUK	It was good. (He scratches his head thoughtfully) Nothing more.
MLLE. SKUNK	The will has been read. There's nothing for you. You're not mentioned.
GLAZIER	Let's strike a blow! Strike a blow!
DR. PIOUK	Marguerite, you'd think was — (he searches) raffia.
GLAZIER	(To Mlle. Skunk) You're being calm.
MLLE. SKUNK	Oh, there is nothing to fear. It's all arranged. You haven't told him anything?
GLAZIER	We are now aware of the motives for his behavior. They escape me for the moment, but I dare say I could reconstruct them if it happens to be of interest to you. (Pause) We are aware as well of the goal that he's been pursuing, for two years. He defined it in unforgettable terms, and nonetheless I forget them. (Pause) And we know — (To Doctor Piouk who mumbles and can't sit still) quiet! — we know — brace yourselves — are you bracing yourselves? — be ready for a shock — we know —

	(Pause) — that he's no longer pursuing it. (A silence) What a coup! (Violently) Why, you mean to tell me you don't understand?
MLLE. SKUNK	Not very well.
GLAZIER	Why, you're utterly dense!
MLLE. SKUNK	I'm tired.
DR. PIOUK	Without being sated. Classic souvenir.
GLAZIER	He's giving up. It's over. He made a mistake! He's beaten. On the ropes. Done for! Knocked out! He owns up. Ask him.
MLLE. SKUNK	It's true, Victor? Oh say that it's true!
GLAZIER	He saw his father last night. That finished him off. I always said we'd get him that way.
MLLE. SKUNK	Victor! My love! It's over? You're done for? Oh, how delightful!
VICTOR	What?
MLLE. SKUNK	You don't want to live like this anymore? Say that it's quite true!
DR. PIOUK	Silence! Enough! Let's finish up! To work! Give-and-take! Lights! (The Glazier turns on the light. Dr. Piouk gets nearer to Victor, looks at him close up) Funny-looking mug.
MLLE. SKUNK	Maybe now —
DR. PIOUK	Silence! Silence when I'm work-

	ing! (To Victor) Monsieur, I will be brief. You don't want to live. Do you have a desire to die? (He raises his hand) Stop and think.
VICTOR	What business is it of yours?
DR. PIOUK	Be straightforward. Don't be afraid. Loosen up. This is a unique opportunity.
VICTOR	Who told you I didn't want to live? What do you know about it? What do you call that? (He puts forth his trembling hand) The wind in the reeds?
DR. PIOUK	Monsieur, I joined your gloom-ridden family through the work-ings of marriage. Odd workings. For the forty-eight hours that I've been inside the metropolis, I've been hearing only about you. Idiocies. I listen. I draw my con-clusions. I see one thing only: distress. I come running. I see you. Smart boy, hypersensitive, great independence of character, health robust, at any rate not one lesion, incapable of shuffling, is trying to find his way. Vital signs reduced to a minimum. For what purpose? That's of no interest to me. I see tendency, movement. What's at issue? (Pause) Monsieur, a man like yourself, so long as he doesn't have three grams of

morphine in his hand, tosses
about in the void. (Pause) You
reject my terms? No! The purest
act of consciousness, the most
sublime flight, is howlingly (He
takes his head in his hands)
physical, howlingly, you know it as
well as I do, it's engraved on your
comedones. (Pause) This is rigor-
ously pain-free, you'll see, you will
not have a moment's discomfort.

VICTOR   I don't see what interest —

DR. PIOUK   You're really intent on knowing
that? Such a trifle? No. You are
shilly-shallying. Quite simply.
Listen to me. Humankind — (He
turns slightly toward the audience,
clears his throat, takes an
announcer's tone) — a few per-
sonal impressions regarding man.
Ahem! At the very top of the list
there are the rubs. It's over, he
doesn't get any further. And
another thing: his state revolts
him, more or less. It's too much
and it's too little. But he is re-
signed to it, for he bears resigna-
tion inside him, that of time's
night, bold-faced ellipsis! If he
could leave it at that! Submitting
to his condition! But no. He
speaks well of it. He sings its
praises! He casts it behind the

ozone! He leaves it behind reluctantly! Ah, the bastard! He ends up preferring himself to the moles, to moss. It's sickening! (Pause) And to close, a thing that I've often noticed: he breeds! For the sake of breeding! (To Victor, passionately) Don't be like them! Don't let yourself be pushed around! Don't do as so many young hopefuls, slipping away, slipping away, vanishing. Badly put, of no importance whatsoever. So then, the great refusal, not the little one, the great one, of which man alone is capable, the most glorious thing of which he is capable, the refusal to be! (Wipes his forehead)

MLLE. SKUNK	Take it easy, take it easy.
GLAZIER	My goodness, he's all worked up. What a gift of gab! You'd think he works on commission.
DR. PIOUK	(He digs around in his pocket, takes out a tablet, holds it straight out for a moment between thumb and forefinger) Freedom!
GLAZIER	The swine! He does find the words that are needed.
DR. PIOUK	Take it! (He proffers the tablet to Victor who takes it, gets up, goes under the light. Mlle. Skunk follows him anxiously)

Mlle. Skunk	(To Dr. Piouk who hasn't budged) Doctor!
Glazier	Careful!
Victor	(Reading) Aspirin *du Rhône.* You must think I'm a complete idiot!
Dr. Piouk	(Rushing over) What? (He hastily takes back the tablet, looks at it) He's right! What a birdbrain! (He hits his head) This one's for me. (He swallows it) The old, the cowardly, the bastards, the scum of the earth, the washouts, for them the aspirins. But for *you* — (He digs around in his pocket) — for you the young, the pure, the lads of the future — (He takes out the tablet, the good one) — we have something different — (He displays the tablet) — something altogether different! By your leave. (He takes Victor's hand, places the tablet in it) Delightful moment! Such a warm hand, so alive! (Solicitously) You have a temperature?
Victor	(Looking at the tablet) It's swallowed?
Dr. Piouk	It is not a suppository, Monsieur.
Glazier	Careful! Careful!
Mlle. Skunk	Victor, give me that!
Dr. Piouk	With a little running water, as much as possible.

VICTOR	What's the guarantee?
DR. PIOUK	Of what?
VICTOR	Of effectiveness.
DR. PIOUK	The word of a professional, Monsieur, and of an honest man. Look at me! (Victor looks at him) You've looked into these eyes? There's your guarantee.
VICTOR	I believe you.
DR. PIOUK	Thank you.
VICTOR	You could pay dearly.
DR. PIOUK	What difference can that make to you?
VICTOR	None, obviously, I seek to understand.
GLAZIER	He too! Some hash!
DR. PIOUK	(Angrily) Oh, you're all the same! Give that back to me. (He extends his hand)
VICTOR	I'm keeping it. I'm going to think it out. (Pause) No, I'll be frank with you, it's all thought out. I don't need it. I'm keeping it all the same.
GLAZIER	And there you have it. Congratulations all around. (To Mlle. Skunk) Here you are happy at last, you'll just have to lay hold of it during his sleep, his sleep of the spent, you'll flush it away, with the rest.

DR. PIOUK	I'm disgusted with myself. (Pause) Deeply so.
GLAZIER	Me too, I'm disgusted with you.
MLLE. SKUNK	(Taking Victor by the arm) Come!
GLAZIER	What composure! What self-assurance!
DR. PIOUK	She's slightly frigid.
VICTOR	Come? Where?
MLLE. SKUNK	(Exaltedly) With me! To meet up with life! Hand in hand! Dawn is breaking!
GLAZIER	Our time here is ended. Of the consolations of quack medicine you want no part. So, go! With her, since she's here. You'll go a little ways together.
DR. PIOUK	Marry her! Knock her up! Take your pleasure, take leave of your senses, come to your senses, writhe, croak!
VICTOR	It's all a mistake. I'm staying here. (A silence)
MLLE. SKUNK	But — !
VICTOR	(Jerky delivery) I've changed my mind. (A silence) Two years, it's too little. (Pause) A life, it's too little. (Pause) My life will be long and horrible. (Pause) But less horrible than yours. (Pause) I'll never be free. (Pause) But I'll feel myself ceaselessly becoming so. (Pause) My life, I'm going to tell

	you with what I'll be using it up: with grating my chains against each other. From morning to night and night to morning. That useless little sound, that will be my life. I don't say my joy. Joy, that I leave to you. My calm. My limbo. (Pause) And you come to speak to me of love, of reason, of death! (Pause) Hey, look, go away, go away!
DR. PIOUK	What is this thing all about? (To Mlle. Skunk) Do you want me to make out a certification of insanity?
GLAZIER	Talk about a view from every angle, this one comes full circle, and then some. (Pause) I don't know any more what I wanted, but I wouldn't be surprised if I had it.
MLLE. SKUNK	It's all over.
GLAZIER	(Worried, to Victor) You're not going to pull another fast one on us by changing your mind?
VICTOR	What?
DR. PIOUK	It's schizophrenia.
MLLE. SKUNK	Let's go.
GLAZIER	You're right, he's gone.
MLLE. SKUNK	(To the Glazier) You think that he may still change his mind?
GLAZIER	I don't think so. But I am always mistaken. (To Victor) Will you

	motion to her if you change your mind again? (A silence. The Glazier takes Victor by the arm) How about it!
VICTOR	What is it?
GLAZIER	Will you motion to the young lady if you again change your mind?
VICTOR	Yes, yes, I will motion to her.
GLAZIER	(To Mlle. Skunk) You see, he will motion to you. (Pause) Don't cry!
DR. PIOUK	For the love of Saint Anne, let's get out of this hell-hole. I have an awful thirst. (A silence) I'm inviting you out to dinner.
GLAZIER	You're inviting me out to dinner?
DR. PIOUK	Both of you.
GLAZIER	Why me?
DR. PIOUK	I like my revels to be well-attended. After you'll bring me back by taxi.
GLAZIER	Impossible. I have to take care of Michel.
DR. PIOUK	Michel?
GLAZIER	My son. He is ill.
DR. PIOUK	Well then, we'll stop off first and see your son. We'll give him a small sedative. Then we'll go have ourselves a blowout. But handled with care. All three of us. (Pause) Oysters, I have this unbelievable yen for oysters!

GLAZIER	Nothing like the medical men for dancing on graves.
DR. PIOUK	What do you expect me to do? To tear off my moustache? Let's get a move on.
GLAZIER	(To Mlle. Skunk) Don't cry. He'll get over it.
MLLE. SKUNK	Adieu, Victor.
DR. PIOUK	Come. (He draws Olga toward the door) We'll find some other way. (He turns around) I'm in this lucidity phase, it's tremendous. It calls for a drink. (Exit Mlle. Skunk and Dr. Piouk. Victor standing, as if frozen. The Glazier gets closer to him)
GLAZIER	You're not holding it against me? (A silence) I did all I could. I'm leaving you my card. (He proffers his card. Victor doesn't take it, perhaps doesn't see it. The Glazier places it on the bed) Give me your hand. (A silence) Victor!
VICTOR	What is it?
GLAZIER	I'm leaving. Give me your hand.
VICTOR	My hand. Here. (He holds out his hand. The Glazier takes it, shakes it, kisses it, lets go of it, rushes out. Victor looks at his hand still poised, raises, opens and looks at the other, sees the tablet, tosses it aside, rubs one hand against the

other, takes off his shoes using his feet, walks. After a while he sits down on the bed. He sees the glass, tosses it aside. He gets up, goes to the switch, turns it off, goes back and sits down on the bed. Looks at the bed. Sees the Glazier's card, takes it, looks at it, tosses it aside. Fixes the covers. Hears steps. Enter Mme. Karl. She turns on the light)

MME. KARL   Well?

VICTOR   What is it?

MME. KARL   This is how you're going out.

VICTOR   Yes, this is how. What do you want?

MME. KARL   I want my answer. Are you staying or are you leaving? I have three blokes after the room.

VICTOR   I am staying.

MME. KARL   Then give me cash. (Victor gets up, digs around in his trouser pocket, takes out a wad of crumpled bills, gives them to Mme. Karl, digs around again in his pocket, takes out some change, gives it to Mme. Karl. She counts up. Sound of computation) A hundred forty sous are missing.

VICTOR   That's all I have.

MME. KARL   This doesn't cover it.

VICTOR	I'll give it to you another time. (Pause) Take the tools. Sell them. It has to be worth something.
MME. KARL	The tools? What tools? (She sees them, goes and has a closer look at them) But it's not yours, this.
VICTOR	He gave them to me.
MME. KARL	Tell me another! Why would he have given them to you?
VICTOR	I don't know. He gave them to me. Take them. (He sees the Glazier's card, picks it up, gives it to Mme. Karl) Here's his card. You just have to ask him. (Mme. Karl puts the card in her pocket, picks up the tools, puts them in the box)
MME. KARL	How low the ground is! (She gets up again, the box under her arm)
VICTOR	If you find the diamond, keep it for him. He wants it.
MME. KARL	The diamond? What line are you giving me this time? (A silence) What diamond?
VICTOR	I don't know. It's a sort of tool, I believe. Ask someone. (Mme. Karl looks at him, shrugs, goes) Madame Karl. (She turns around) You wouldn't have found a jacket on the stairs?
MME. KARL	A jacket? What jacket?
VICTOR	I can't find my jacket. I believe I

	lost it on the stairs. If you find it you can sell it too. (Pause) It's maroon, I believe.
MME. KARL	Are you sure you're not completely daft? (Victor goes back to sit on his bed. He looks at the covers. Mme. Karl looks at him)
VICTOR	Mme. Karl.
MME. KARL	What?
VICTOR	Mme. Karl.
MME. KARL	WHAT?
VICTOR	You wouldn't have a second cover to give me?
MME. KARL	Why? You're cold in the bed?
VICTOR	Yes.
MME. KARL	Well, soon it will be spring. (A silence) You want to eat?
VICTOR	No.
MME. KARL	I have a nice soup. (A silence) A small *tartine*? (A silence) You are going to get sick. (A silence) It's not me who will be able to nurse you. (A silence) What a sorry sight! (Exit) (Victor seated on the bed. He looks at the bed, the room, the window, the door. He gets up and undertakes to push his bed to the back of the room, as far from the door and the window as possible, that is, toward the side of the footlights with the Audience

member's stage-box. He has a
hard time. He pushes it, pulls it,
with pauses for rest, seated on the
edge of the bed. It is clear that he
is not strong. He finally succeeds.
He sits down on the bed, now
parallel to the footlights. After a
while, he gets up, goes to the
switch, turns it off, looks out the
window, goes back and sits down
on the bed, facing the audience.
He looks perseveringly at the
audience, the orchestra, the
balcony (Should there be one), to
the right, to the left. Then he gets
into bed, his scrawny back turned
on mankind)

CURTAIN

NOTES

p. 15   Impasse de l'Enfant-Jésus. Alley-like street on the left bank, in Paris, located right off the Rue de Vaugirard and between the Boulevard du Montparnasse and the Boulevard Pasteur. Not far from the Luxembourg Gardens and the various faculties of the University of Paris.

p. 16   Passy. According to the Michelin guide, a calm residential neighborhood (16th *arrondissement*) where tall buildings give way to villas and gardens. Debussy, Fauré and Manet are buried in its cemetery, which is about ten blocks from rue Spontini.

p. 17   *Nimis sero, imber serotinus.* May be translated as "too late, the belated showers."

p. 18   The ninth. The ninth (and lowest) circle in the funnel-shaped cavity that is Dante's hell, and home to its worst offenders: the treacherous to (in ascending order of heinousness) kindred, country and cause, guests, and lords and benefactors.

p. 21   Rue Spontini. Fashionable street on the right bank, in Paris, located a few streets away from the Bois de Boulogne, between Avenue Foch and Avenue Victor-

Hugo. About a mile and a half from Victor's Impasse.

p. 27   Delage. Luxury car. After Louis Delage (1874-1947), French industrialist and engineer, and one of the pioneers of the automobile industry. He invented several types of engines.

p. 45   Robinson. (Plessis-Robinson). Suburban center southwest of Paris, chief town (*chef-lieu*) of the canton of Hauts-de-Seine.

p. 113   Iassy. Romanian city, in Moldavia.

p. 120   *Tartine.* Slice of bread usually covered with butter, jam, etc. Half of a *baguette.*

p. 132   Might have known. Involves a somewhat untranslatable play on the use of the Proust-redolent imperfect subjunctive, an exquisitely fussy mood.

p. 147   Taylorizing. After Frederick Winslow Taylor (1856-1915), principal advocate of the scientific management movement in the early twentieth century. Taylor put forth three principals for so reorganizing the workplace as to increase profitability: (a) greater division of labor; (b) complete managerial control of the workplace; and (c) cost-accounting. Taylor believed that with employee motivation being determined by financial considerations, the feeling that they were sharing in the increased profitability produced by workplace reorganization would lead employees to greater cooperation with management. Taylor's emphasis on the suppression of useless gestures must have had a complicated appeal for Beckett the man of the theater.

In large part, as might be expected, companies that adapted scientific management paid no attention to its aim of creating a system of payments involving profit-sharing. It is also believed that in the name of simplifying the gestural economy of the workplace, scientific management as practiced robbed workers of the opportunity to make use of their professional knowledge, their qualifications, and their initiative.

p. 148   *Béquet.* In typography, a small strip of writing added to a proof. Or, more to the point here, a small part of a scene that an author either adds or alters during rehearsals.

p. 149   Canebière. Well-known avenue (Marseilles) leading to the port.

p. 150   Crèvecoeur-sur-Auge. Literally (and Beckett loves these geographical *fantaisies*: cf. Condom-on-the-Baise in *Three Novels*), Heartache-on-the-Trough.

p. 172   *Manille.* Card game where the ten (*manille*) and the ace are the strongest cards. For four players (two against two).

p. 176   Honor to whom honor. Shortened yet completely self-contained form of the

New Testament expression *Honor to whom honor is due* (Romans 13:7), and thus equivalent to Beckett's *A tout seigneur* (the correspondingly autonomous abridgement of *A tout seigneur tout honneur*). Here and, a fortiori, in other instances throughout this work, the translator has tried to remain true to the shape of Beckett's utterance: compressed, close to the bone, warily rationing its lyrical evocation amid the colloquialization of abstract thinking.

p. 182   Aspirin *(Aspirine) du Rhône.* A standard brand of aspirin.